Warehouse Milestones

Englisch für Lagerberufe

von
Dr. Wolfgang Schäfer (Hrsg.)
Annely Humphreys
Jason Humphreys
Arnd Nadolny
Mary Schäfer

Ernst Klett Verlag
Stuttgart · Leipzig

Warehouse Milestones

Englisch für Lagerberufe

Autoren: Dr. Wolfgang Schäfer (Hrsg.), Annely Humphreys, Jason Humphreys, Arnd Nadolny, Mary Schäfer

Werkübersicht:

Schülerbuch, 978-3-12-808284-4
Milestones Workbook für technische Berufe mit Prüfungsvorbereitung KMK-Fremdsprachenzertifikat und Audio-CD-ROM, Übungsbegleitheft für alle technischen Berufe, 978-3-12-808285-1
Milestones Lehrerhandbuch für technische Berufe inkl. Digitalem Lehrer-Service mit Medien-DVD-ROM + Lehrer-Audio-CDs (6), 978-3-12-808287-5

1. Auflage

1 7 6 5 4 3 | 25 24 23 22 21

Im Lehrwerk befinden sich ausschließlich fiktive Internet-Adressen, die deshalb auch mit ww#. beginnen anstatt wie üblich mit www.
Die im Buch abgedruckten Mediencodes führen zu interaktiven Zusatzübungen und Hörverständnistexten auf www.klett.de. Die Mediencodes leiten ausschließlich zu optionalen Unterrichtsmaterialien, sie unterliegen nicht dem staatlichen Zulassungsverfahren.

Projektleitung: Matthias Rupp
Redaktion: Dr. Birgit Reinel, Tübingen; Volker Wendland, Helen Smyth
Herstellung: Angelika Lindner

Satz und Gestaltung: Satzkiste, Stuttgart
Umschlaggestaltung: Projektteam des Verlages
Reproduktion: Meyle + Müller Medien-Management, Pforzheim
Druck: Druckhaus Götz GmbH, Ludwigsburg

Printed in Germany
ISBN 978-3-12-808284-4

9 783128 082844

Warehouse Milestones bietet Ihnen praxisorientiertes Fachenglisch für Lagerfachberufe an Berufsschulen, Berufsfachschulen, Fachschulen sowie für technisch ausgerichtete Englischkurse in der Erwachsenenbildung.

Warehouse Milestones im Überblick:

- Konsequente Berücksichtigung neuester Lehrpläne (Lernfelder) sowie durchgängiges Sprachkompetenztraining nach dem Gemeinsamen Europäischen Referenzrahmen (Sprachstufen A2 – B2).
- 16 kompakte vierseitige Module: Fachmodule mit Schwerpunkt auf Fachenglisch wechseln sich mit Modulen (A – H) ab, in denen der Schwerpunkt auf der beruflichen Kommunikation liegt.
- Schnelle Orientierung im Buch durch Übersicht der Lernziele jeweils am Modulanfang.
- Die Kompetenzen auf einen Blick: Viele Aufgaben bereiten bereits gezielt auf die Anforderungen des KMK-Zertifikats hin. Diese Aufgaben sind mit den Kürzeln R (Rezeption), P (Produktion), I (Interaktion) und M (Mediation) gekennzeichnet.
- Typische Sprachhandlungssituationen im Berufsalltag werden multimedial mit Audio- und Videounterstützung (u. a. Originalvideos der BBC) trainiert.
- Zahlreiche Partner-, Gruppen- und Internetaufgaben werden durch Texte und Aufgaben zur Arbeitssicherheit *(Safety first)* abgerundet.
- In den Modulen befinden sich hilfreiche Verweise auf die nach beruflichen Situationen geordneten Redewendungen *(Phrases)*.
- Unter der Überschrift *Understanding technical English* befinden sich Hinweise und Aufgaben zum richtigen Umgang mit englischem Fachvokabular.
- Möglichkeit zur Binnendifferenzierung durch anspruchsvollere Aufgaben sowie Aufgaben zur Vorbereitung auf das KMK-Fremdsprachenzertifikat auf verschiedenen Stufen.
- Auf den Fachwortschatz in den jeweiligen Modulen kann über die *Word bank* (auf jeder Doppelseite) direkt zugegriffen werden.
- Online-Grammatiktraining über die Milestones-Codes 🌐 3u5mw9 in den Modulen A – H.
- Vertieftes Grammatik- und Hörverstehenstraining im Workbook mit Prüfungsvorbereitung auf das KMK-Fremdsprachenzertifikat, inklusive Audio-CD-ROM mit allen technischen Milestones-Fachbänden- und Workbook-Audios (MP3).

Weiterführendes Material

Milestones Workbook für technische Berufe mit Prüfungsvorbereitung KMK-Fremdsprachenzertifikat und Audio-CD-ROM

Lehrerhandbuch für alle technischen Milestones-Fachbände mit 6 Audio-CDs + Digitaler Lehrer-Service (Lehrer-Software mit multimedialen Schülerbüchern, Audios, Videos, Lösungen, Übungsmaterial, Übungsgenerator, Dokumentenpool mit veränderbaren Materialien)

Videos, Anhang, Symbole ▶

Üben interaktiv: Online Grammatiktraining

Modul A: 3u5mw9	**Modul E:** 5zw8jx
Modul B: gc2x9w	**Modul F:** pf5r3n
Modul C: x3gj95	**Modul G:** 3b9c4h
Modul D: cy8yn5	**Modul H:** 842j42

Die Module A – H legen den Schwerpunkt auf die Skills zu Business Communication, die im Workbook intensiv trainiert werden.

Video lounge (Die Videos und die Videoskripte befinden sich im Lehrerhandbuch.) 72

V 1 Company tour

V 2 Telephoning

V 3 Job interview

V 4 Technical support

V 5 Waste – the future's most valuable resource

V 6 Pipe inspection

V 7 High voltage work

V 8 Ras Laffan

V 9 Pipelines

V 10 Robots in the hospital

V 11 Portable power stations

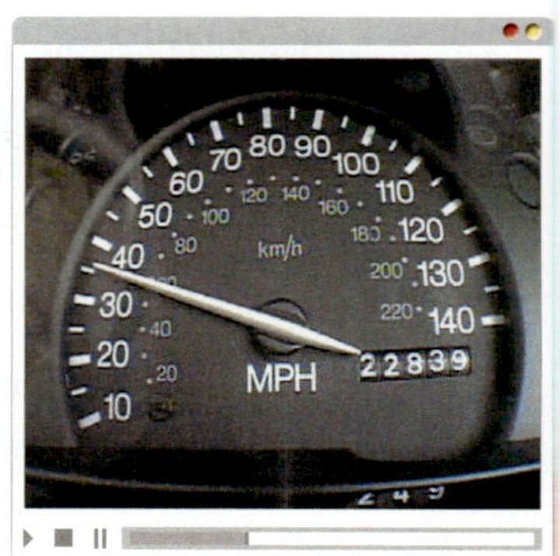

V 12 Car speed control

Appendix

Umschlagseiten

Modulelemente

Nach diesem Modul	Lernziele
WORD BANK	Fachvokabular
UNDERSTANDING TECHNICAL ENGLISH	Hinweise und Aufgaben zu englischem Fachvokabular
SAFETY FIRST ⚠	Aufgaben zur Arbeitssicherheit
→ **PHRASES:** Telephoning	Verweis auf *Phrases (Telephoning)* im Anhang

Symbole

◎ A 1.2	Audioverweis mit Tracknummer (CD1 – Track 2)
P, M, I, R	Produktion, Mediation, Interaktion, Rezeption
🌐	Aufgabe mit Internetrecherche
▲	Anspruchsvollere Aufgabe *(advanced)*
👥	Partner- und Gruppenaufgaben
🌐 3u5mw9	Grammatiktraining online über www.klett.de
KMK II	Aufgabe zur Vorbereitung auf die Prüfung des KMK-Fremdsprachenzertifikats (Niveaustufe II)

01

NACH DIESEM MODUL:

- ✓ kann ich auf Englisch den Ablauf am Wareneingang beschreiben,
- ✓ kann ich die Dokumente beim Erhalt von Waren auf Englisch verstehen,
- ✓ kann ich auf Englisch mangelhafte Ware reklamieren.

1

2

3

4

Receiving and checking goods

Lots of different products from many countries are stored in warehouses. The warehouse is the transfer point of goods where the supplier's transportation contract ends. He or she hands over the goods to the warehouse workers and transfers the ownership of the goods to them.

1 **Read the steps that are taken when goods arrive at a warehouse. Then match the descriptions in the box to the steps 1–5.**

documentation check • quality and quantitative check • quay parking • unloading goods • integration of goods into stock

1. The truck driver is directed to a dock so that the goods can be unloaded.
2. The goods are unloaded from the truck at the receiving dock by the driver or warehouse workers. Heavy goods are put on conveyor belts.
3. The number of the packages is checked. The packages are also checked for damage and if the products are the right ones.
4. The delivery documents are checked against the order.
5. The goods are taken into stock using a barcode scanner.

2 **Look at the photos and describe them to your partner.**

A | People and departments involved in receiving goods

Different people and departments are involved in the process of receiving goods when they arrive at the warehouse.

1 Look at the table and decide which definitions go with which departments or people. Then form complete sentences.

1. supplier	is the person	who	is responsible for taking and checking goods
2. purchasing department	is the department	which	has to deliver goods in perfect condition
3. receiving department	is the company		orders goods and can help receiving staff when there is a problem with a delivery
4. quality department			is responsible for the transportation of goods and any damage to or loss of goods during transport
5. transportation company			checks that goods meet the specifications agreed when the order was placed

2 Look at exercise 1 again and find the English meanings of the words and phrases below.

1. Warenannahme
2. Einkauf(sabteilung)
3. Spedition
4. verantwortlich für
5. Beschädigung
6. den vereinbarten Bedingungen entsprechen

M/I **3** Führen Sie den folgenden Dialog zwischen zwei Auszubildenden auf Englisch.

Partner A	Partner B
Fragen Sie Partner B in welcher Abteilung er/sie arbeitet.	
	Sagen Sie, dass Sie in der Warenannahme arbeiten.
Fragen Sie nach den Aufgaben, die Partner B dort zu erledigen hat.	
	Sagen Sie, dass Sie für das Annehmen und Überprüfen von Waren verantwortlich sind.
Fragen Sie, ob Partner B mit dem Einkauf zusammenarbeitet.	
	Sagen Sie, dass der Einkauf Ihnen beim Verlust oder im Falle einer Beschädigung von Waren hilft. Erkundigen Sie sich danach in welcher Abteilung Partner A arbeitet und was seine/ihre Aufgaben sind.
Sagen Sie, dass Sie in der Qualitätsabteilung arbeiten. Teilen Sie weiterhin mit, dass es Ihre Aufgabe ist zu überprüfen, dass die Waren den vereinbarten Bedingungen entsprechen.	

→ **PHRASES:** Your company

WORD BANK

barcode scanner – Strichcodeleser
contract – Vertrag
conveyor belt – Förderband, Transportband
delivery document – Lieferpapier
documentation check – Dokumentenüberprüfung
goods – Waren
integration of goods – Warenaufnahme
quality department – Qualitätsabteilung
quay parking – Parken am richtigen Ablageort
receiving dock – Empfangsrampe
receiving staff – Personal zuständig für den Lagereingang
stock – Lager, Lagerbestand
store (v) – (ein)lagern
supplier – Lieferant, Zulieferer
take into stock – auf Lager nehmen
transfer ownership – das Eigentum übertragen
transfer point – Übergabepunkt
warehouse – Lager(haus)
warehouse worker – Lagerarbeiter(in)

B | Receiving documentation

1 **Complete the information about the receiving documentation using the words in the box. Two of the words are not needed.**

> customer • warehouse workers • supplier • carrier • quality department

The delivery note which is issued by the **1** lists all of the delivered goods. The transportation bill is issued by the **2** who gives the truck driver the task of transporting the goods. Finally, we have the receiving note, which is used by the **3** to check that a delivery corresponds with the order.

R **2** ⦾ A 3.16 **Jan Kowalski, an English truck driver has just brought a delivery to a warehouse in Bremen. Listen to the dialogue and answer the questions.**

1. What does the warehouse worker find out when he checks the goods?
2. What does Jan Kowalski ask the warehouse worker to do?
3. What do you have to do in the presence of the driver when you notice a problem during a first visual check? Describe the steps.

R **3** ⦾ A 3.16 **Listen to the dialogue again and write down the missing information in the delivery note (a – f) on a separate sheet of paper.**

DELIVERY NOTE

Gusto Coffee Machines
15 Langston Road, Birmingham, NE2 2RS

To:	Paul Steiner GmbH	**Order number:**	a
Address:	Am Ringbrunnen 23	**Dispatch date:**	b
	28198 Bremen	**Invoice number:**	c
		Contact person:	Jill Cameron
Attention:	Gerd Wolters	**Email:**	d

Quantity delivered:	**Product description:**
e	Type Meldiva – 6 coffee machines per package
Comments: f	

Signature: *Jill Cameron*

Date: 18.01.20...

P **4** **List things that could go wrong with a delivery. Compare your list with others and add ideas to your list.**

P **5** **Find out what you should do when problems arise during the secondary check of a delivery. Search the Internet for information and present your results to the class.**

C | Barcode scanners

M **1** KMK I

Da für ein neues Lager demnächst Scanner angeschafft werden sollen, hat Ihr Vorgesetzter im Internet Informationen über mobile Barcode Scanner gesucht. Er hat folgenden englischen Text gefunden und bittet Sie, die wichtigsten Punkte für ihn auf Deutsch festzuhalten. Schreiben Sie diese Zusammenfassung.

ww#.scanning_goods.com

Instructions to follow when scanning delivered goods

1 ....

Point the mobile barcode scanner with the red scanning light at the barcode on the package.

2 ....

Engage the scanner, if necessary. Some scanners, however, read the barcode automatically and do not have to be engaged. In all other cases make sure that the red light is lined up with the barcode and then press the engage button. This button can normally be found on the back of a mobile scanner.

3 ....

After all of the new items have been scanned, connect the barcode scanner to a monitor in order to see if all items have been scanned correctly. If the monitor does not display the correct items, you must scan them again.

2 **UNDERSTANDING TECHNICAL ENGLISH**

1. **The following pairs of words are often mixed up. Find their German equivalents in a dictionary.**

   warehouse/department store • actual/current •
   conveyor belt/assembly line • to check/to control

2. **Complete the sentences using the correct words in the exercise above.**
   a. When I need to buy a number of things, I usually go to a ? in town.
   b. Factory workers make products on an ? .
   c. The ? number of packages in the warehouse is 6,280 in total.
   d. Warehouse workers visually ? a delivery of goods.
   e. Products are stored in a ? .
   f. Lots of computers ? the processes in a warehouse.
   g. The ? price we have got to pay for the goods is much higher than we expected.
   h. A ? is used to transport heavy goods from one place to another in a warehouse.

WORD BANK

carrier – Spediteur, Frachtführer
delivery note – Lieferschein
receiving note – Empfangsbescheinigung
transportation bill – Transportschein, -liste

WORD BANK ◎

countersign (v) – gegenzeichnen
invoice number – Rechnungsnummer
item – Posten, Artikel
label – Aufkleber, Aufschrift
make out (v) – ausstellen
order number – Auftragsnummer

A

NACH DIESEM MODUL:

- ✓ weiß ich, wie man sich auf Englisch begrüßt,
- ✓ weiß ich, wie ich mich selbst und andere einander auf Englisch vorstelle.

1

2

3

4

Meeting people

In the world of work you will often meet new people and it will be necessary to introduce yourself. In all industries developing relationships with colleagues and customers is the key to success. Not only is it important that you are polite, confident and friendly, but also that you know what to say, what information to include, and what the differences between formal and informal situations are.

1 **Match the parts of the dialogues to form short conversations. Start with Speaker A.**

Speaker A	Speaker B
1. Morning, Tom. That was a great game last night, wasn't it?	a. Nice to meet you, too, Hannah.
2. Hi guys, my name's Natalie.	b. Goodbye, Mr Horvath. It was nice meeting you.
3. Goodbye, Mr Bauer. See you next week.	c. Morning Chris. Yeah, it was amazing!
4. It's nice to meet you, Simon.	d. Hi Natalie, I'm Mark. Welcome to the team.

2 **Now match the conversations above with the appropriate picture (1–4) and decide which are formal and which are informal.**

P **3** **Which other phrases do you know for greeting somebody and saying goodbye? Make a list.**

A | Saying "hello" and "goodbye" and giving your name

A trainee from Denmark has just arrived at Neureuther und Söhne in Kiel for a three-month internship.

R **1** ⊚ A 1.1 **Listen to the two dialogues and write down the names of the people and their positions in the company.**

R **2** ⊚ A 1.1 **Listen again and write down the phrases the people use for greeting and introducing one another.**

R **3** **Match the replies to the greetings and goodbyes in the two boxes.**

Formal greetings / goodbyes	Formal replies
1. Good morning. How are you today?	a. Good morning. I'm fine, thanks. And you?
2. Good night. Have a nice evening, Mr Dachs.	b. Goodbye, Mr Schäfer, and thanks for everything.
3. Goodbye, Mr Horvath. Have a nice journey home.	c. Good night, Ms Kistner, you too.
4. Good night, Silke.	d. Good night, Ms Hornbach.

Informal greetings / goodbyes	Informal replies
1. Hello, Mike. Haven't seen you for a long time.	a. Bye, Thomas. Give me a call, will you?
2. Lena, how are you this morning?	b. You, too, Florian. Thank you.
3. Morning. How was your weekend?	c. Fine, thanks. How about yours?
4. Bye-bye, Sevda.	d. I'm good, thanks. Yourself?
5. Have a nice weekend, Joe.	e. Yes, I was away on a trip last week.

P **4** **Make dialogues from the following prompts and present them to the class. Look at your lists of phrases from exercise 2 and check the info box on the next page.**

Example:
A: Hello, my name is Marina Kohler. I represent Toolcell in Leipzig.
B: Hello, Ms Kohler. I'm Amy Strong from Easytools in Bern. Nice to meet you.
A: Nice to meet you, too, Ms Strong.

Names: Denise Hofmann • Marina Kohler • Alice Campbell • Abel Kazich • Tanja Neuhäuser • Rudolfo Orvieto • Ursula Braun • Stefan Helm • Gerard Mathieu • your name

Job descriptions: I'm a trainee / intern • I work for … • I come from … • I represent … • I'm training to be a … • your job

Companies: Toolcell GmbH in Leipzig, Germany • Easytools in Bern, Switzerland • Tools Expert Pontypridd, Wales • DWT Electronics, Stuttgart • Smart EDV, Kiel • Xiang Piong Ltd, Hong Kong • Naturholz GmbH • your company

Situations: a first meeting with a new customer • a meeting with an existing customer / a colleague • a party • a company open day • a trade fair • a job fair for trainees • the first day in a new company

WORD BANK ⊚

intern – Praktikant(in)

5 Introduce the people to each other according to the following structure. Use the prompts on the previous page.

→ **PHRASES:** Meeting people

A: Fragen Sie **B** und **C**, ob sie sich schon kennen. B und C antworten mit Nein.
A: Stellen Sie **B** und **C** einander vor.

B: Begrüßen Sie **C** freundlich.

C: Sie grüßen **B** zurück und stellen eine Frage zu **Bs** Firma

B: Sie geben eine Auskunft über Ihre Firma. Sie fragen **C** nach seiner Tätigkeit.

C: Sie beantworten **Bs** Frage.

INFO BOX: Meeting people

First meeting / Formal introduction

A: Hello, my name is Ines Sacher.
B: Nice to meet you, Ms Sacher. My name is Joshua Hamsung.
A: Nice to meet you, too, Mr Hamsung.
Women – married or not – are addressed as Ms, not Miss.

A: Mr Jacobs, this is Mr Sykes.
B: How do you do?
C: How do you do?
"How do you do?" is rarely used for first introductions.

A: I'm Frank Warren of Wood Tools in Manchester. Please call me Frank.
B: Pleased to meet you, Frank. My name is Joanne McNeill. Do call me Joanne.
In English-speaking countries first names are often used from the start of a business realtionship. In South America or Asia, however, you don't usually use first names right away.

I hope you had a good trip. /
I hope you had no trouble finding us. /
Welcome to our stand.
Phrases like these are used to break the ice after an introduction.

Second meeting

A: Good morning, Ms Sacher. Do you remember me? I'm Joshua Hamsung from Bell & Co in Chicago.
B: Good morning, Mr Hamsung. Nice to see you again.

Informal meetings

A: Hello Ines. Great to see you again. How are you?
B: Hi Joshua. Lovely to see you, too. I'm fine. And you?

B | Intercultural awareness

M **1**
KMK II

Ihr Betrieb wird in Zukunft für einen amerikanischen Auftraggeber arbeiten. Ihre Vorgesetzte interessiert sich daher für folgenden Artikel aus einer englischen Fachzeitschrift. Sie bittet Sie, die wesentlichen Aussagen des Artikels stichpunktartig in übersichtlicher Form für sie auf Deutsch herauszuarbeiten.

Intercultural awareness

Politeness, pleasantries and profitability

Americans are known to be direct, but they do like to take a few minutes to chat before getting down to work. They may ask after your health, or if your trip was pleasant, or about where you are from. This gives both parties a chance to form an impression of the other and establishes a basis on which to do business.

Americans, including the president, like to be called by their given name. This is not an invitation to be personal, as you would expect in Germany if someone suggested using the familiar "Du". It is a way to set a framework for working together. While it is usual in business, it would not be expected in dealing with a doctor, a teacher or a professor, and in any case, you should wait until it is offered: "Hello, I'm James Smith, vice-president in charge of sales. Call me Jim." "Pleased to meet you! I'm Walter König; please call me Walter." (Note that in the United States you state your *given* name and then your *family* name, and not the other way around, except perhaps on a form that you have to fill out.)

Americans don't like to waste time. They get to the point, in conversations as well as in conferences. Although Milton Berle, a comedian from the 1950s and 1960s, is quoted as saying: "A committee is a group of people that keeps minutes and wastes hours."

Americans are generally very polite, and they tend to smile much more than we are used to. An American tourist was quite upset that perfect strangers didn't smile back at her when she walked through the streets of a small town in Germany. On the other hand, a German woman in New York became quite tired of being asked, again by perfect strangers, the person at the cash register, the bus driver: "How are you doing?" and commanded to "Have a nice day!" These pleasantries are intended to show that you are noticed and respected. More than "Thanks!" is not expected.

P **2**

Check the Internet to see what advice people from other countries get to prepare for meetings in Germany. Make a list of ten useful tips.

02

NACH DIESEM MODUL:

- ✓ kann ich auf Englisch unterschiedliche Lagerarten nennen,
- ✓ kann ich auf Englisch Warnschilder und Handhabungssymbole erläutern,
- ✓ kann ich auf Englisch ein Warenwirtschaftssystem beschreiben.

Storing and handling goods

When products are properly organised in the warehouse, they can be located quickly when they are needed. Goods that are not stored correctly can be easily misplaced or damaged. Goods can be stored on pallets, on shelves or in bins. Forklifts are often used to place pallets of goods onto pallet racks.

1 Why is a good storage system important? Choose the correct answer(s).

1. Warehouse workers can find an order quickly.
2. The goods can be lost easily.
3. The goods are not damaged so quickly.

2 Complete the dialogue between the workers in the photo. Use the words in the box.

E118 · goods · pallet · rack · shelf · store

Tom: Who left the [1] of bottles here?
Peter: I don't know. Where do you want to [2] them?
Tom: Please place the pallet on the third [3] from the bottom.
Peter: What's the number of the pallet [4]?
Tom: It's [5]. It's important to put the [6] where we can easily find them later.

A | Storage facilities

Every product needs the correct storage facilities so that it can be stored and transported safely and any damage to it can be avoided. Valuable products that should be protected from sunlight are often stored in boxes or crates. Food is mostly stored in shelving racks in supermarkets or on pallet racks in warehouses. Sweets are often put into small bins only. Products made of rubber, however, should not be palletized. The best way of storing them is on shelving racks so they can be lifted out from both sides.

1 Match the words with the photos. One of the words does not match.

shelving racks • pallet racks • wooden boxes • bins

1

2

3

2 Describe the products in the photos above using the words in the box.

easily damaged • individually wrapped • non-palletized • all the same size • different sizes • bulky

R **3** A 3.17 Listen to the dialogue between the head storeman of a Manchester warehouse, Mr Walker, and Frank Löwe. Frank is an apprentice from Hamburg who is doing a work placement in Manchester. Make a table with the products they talk about and the storage facilities used for them.

Products	Storage facilities

R **4** A 3.17 Listen to the dialogue again and say which products are described with the words in exercise 2.

5 Search the Internet for more storage facilities and list them.

P **6** Give a short report about the storage facilities that are used in your company's warehouse.

WORD BANK

bin – Behälter
bulky – sperrig, unhandlich, übergroß
crate – Kiste
damage – Beschädigung, Schaden
forklift – Gabelstapler
handle (v) – handhaben
pallet – Palette
palletize (v) – palettieren, auf eine Palette stapeln
rack – Regal
shelving rack – Fachregal
storage facilities – Lagermöglichkeiten
storage system – Lagersystem
store (v) – (ein)lagern
warehouse – Lager(haus)
wrap (v) – einwickeln, einpacken, umhüllen

WORD BANK

in operation – in Betrieb
warehouse management system – Lagerverwaltungssystem

B | Storing products in the right place

It is important to store products in the right place to keep them in good condition. For example, some products have to be kept in climate controlled storage or humidity controlled storage: the wrong temperature or high humidity levels can damage stock. Hazardous goods, such as gases, must be stored in a well-ventilated, safety controlled space.

1 Give the German words for the types of storage in the photos.

1

Safety controlled storage

2

Temperature controlled storage

3

Humidity controlled storage

2 Complete the sentences with the correct type of storage.

1. Wooden boards have to be kept dry so they are put into ? .
2. Dairy products can spoil so that ? must be used.
3. Liquid chemicals need special ? so that other products are not damaged.

P/I **3** Decide how to store the following products properly. Give reasons.

1. flammable solids
2. meat and fish products
3. electronic goods
4. explosives
5. beer
6. mattresses with metal springs

4 Choose the correct modal auxiliary.

1. Products (needn't/mustn't) be misplaced when they are stored.
2. Heavy products (may/should) be put on pallets before transporting them to the right storage place.
3. You (have to/needn't) be qualified before you are allowed to drive a forklift.
4. (May/Must) warehouse workers wear helmets in the warehouse?

5 UNDERSTANDING TECHNICAL ENGLISH

1. Find the meanings of the word pairs with 'rack' in a dictionary.

   roof rack • luggage rack • bicycle rack • book rack

2. Find two more word pairs with 'rack' and explain their meaning to your partner.

C | Labelling goods

The goods in a warehouse must be labelled with handling symbols so that warehouse workers know how to handle them correctly. The handling symbols are printed on the packaging. Incorrect handling can lead to damage to goods. For example, objects which are made of glass can easily get broken if handled incorrectly.

WORD BANK

handling symbol – Handhabungssymbol
helmet – Helm
humidity – Feuchtigkeit
label (v) – etikettieren, beschriften
packaging – Verpackung(smaterial)
safety controlled – sicherheitsüberwacht
solid – Feststoff
stock – Waren
well-ventilated – gut belüftet
wirelessly – drahtlos

1 **SAFETY FIRST ⚠**
Match the handling symbols with the correct German meaning.

trocken lagern • leicht entflammbar • zerbrechlich • kühl lagern

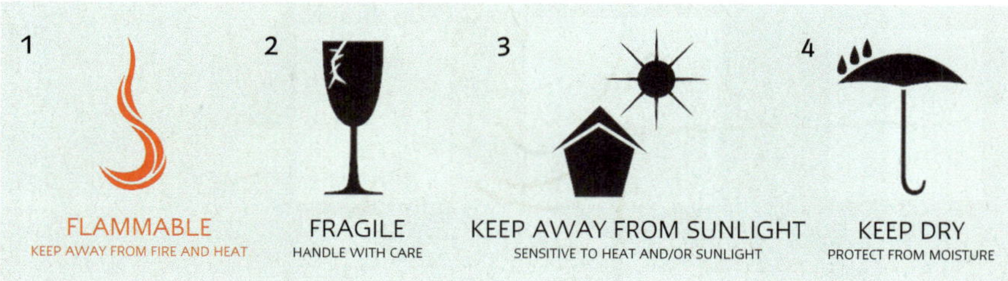

2 **Choose the correct handling symbols for the products.**

perfumes • paper • pianos • food products

R **3** KMK II **Ihr Chef hat in einer englischen Fachzeitschrift einen Artikel über den Einsatz eines Warenwirtschaftssystems zur besseren Lagerverwaltung gefunden. Er bittet Sie diesen Artikel auszuwerten. Beantworten Sie seine Fragen dazu auf Deutsch.**

1. Was versteht man unter einem Warenwirtschaftssystem?
2. Welche Aufgaben übernimmt ein Warenwirtschaftssystem?
3. Wie funktioniert die Übertragung von Daten in den meisten Fällen?
4. Was spricht aus Sicht eines Unternehmens für die Installation eines solchen Systems?

Warehouse management systems

Warehouse management systems (WMS) are best described as the operating processes that optimize all of the functions of a warehouse. The WMS automatically handles the receipt of stock, its storage in the warehouse and returns. This is often done by computers. The transport of products is monitored and information is sent wirelessly to a central database. This provides warehouse staff with information about the quantity of goods in the warehouse or where the products have been stored. The WMS is cost-efficient and helps to optimize stock.

When warehouse workers have up-to-date information, they can work more effectively. In this way costs can be reduced and customer service improved. A good WMS helps a company to manage lots of work in real time.
The WMS is only as good as its software. Software must be reliable, and easy to install and handle. The basic functions of good software include a physical inventory, shipping, receiving and picking, as well as dealing with queries and barcode labelling.

B

NACH DIESEM MODUL:

- ✓ kann ich verschiedene Firmenabteilungen auf Englisch erklären,
- ✓ kann ich Arbeitsplätze und Tätigkeiten auf Englisch beschreiben,
- ✓ kann ich eine Firmenstruktur auf Englisch beschreiben.

1

2

3

4

Your company

Regardless of whether your company builds houses, repairs cars, or makes furniture, there is likely to come a time where you will be required to talk about yourself, your job and your company in English. Whether you are greeting an English-speaking visitor, giving a tour of the factory, or talking to suppliers from another country, it is important you have the skills and vocabulary to express yourself clearly.

1 Work on your own. Look at the photos and brainstorm words that describe what is shown in each of them.

I/P **2** Compare your list of words with your partner and work together to describe the pictures. Use these words to help you:

building site • cable • construction worker • grease • hard hat • car mechanic • overalls • ratchet • server • timber • tools • wires • work gloves

WATCH OUT!

She ~~wears~~ a hard hat. She is wearing a hard hat.

P **3** With your partner, think of three questions you would like to ask each of the four young workers shown in the photos.

A | The company and its departments

P **1** **Use the words and phrases in the table to explain what the departments of Krone Elektronik GmbH do.**

Example: Sales and Marketing advertises and sells the products.

Department		
Sales and Marketing	distribute	the products are not damaged.
Production Planning	*advertise and sell*	new employees.
Accounts	check	raw materials.
HR (Human Resources)	buy	*the products.*
Production	deal with	the computer network.
Logistics	recruit and train	the finished products.
Purchasing	maintain	customer problems.
Customer Service	handle	the company's finances.
R&D (Research and Development)	make	new products.
IT (Information Technology)	organize	production schedules.
Quality Control	develop	the products to the customers.

P **2** **Use the information in the table to form sentences using *responsible for / in charge of*.**

Example:
The Production department is responsible for making the products.
The Production Planning department is in charge of …

P **3** **Look at the departments again and write down three questions. Then close your book and ask your partner.**

Example:
A: What is the Quality Control department responsible for?
B: It is responsible for …
A: Which department is in charge of …?
B: The … department is in charge of …

R **4** KMK I ◎A 1.2 **Der Ausbildungsleiter von Krone Elektronik, Herr Kirchner, zeigt Sean, einem Elektrotechnikstudenten aus Belfast, das Firmengelände und die einzelnen Abteilungen. Hören Sie sich das Gespräch an und beantworten Sie die folgenden Fragen auf Deutsch.**

1. Wann wurde Krone Elektronik GmbH gegründet, und von wem?
2. Wo hat die Firma ihren Hauptsitz?
3. Wie viele Produktionsanlagen hat Krone Elektronik insgesamt?
4. Wo wird nächstes Jahr eine neue Produktionsanlage eröffnet?
5. Wie viele Leute beschäftigt die Firma?
6. Woran arbeitet die Forschungs- und Entwicklungsabteilung gerade?
7. Welche drei Abteilungen befinden sich in dem Hauptgebäude?
8. Wo wird Sean zuerst arbeiten?
9. Wie viele Zylinderköpfe werden jährlich bei Krone Elektronik hergestellt?
10. Was passiert momentan in der IT-Abteilung?

WORD BANK

grease – Fett, Schmierfett
ratchet – Knarre
raw materials – Rohmaterialien
recruit (v) – anwerben
tool – Werkzeug

B | Tasks and responsibilities

Industrial companies are made up of many different people, who all have a variety of tasks and responsibilities. DWG Tech GmbH in Stuttgart manufactures machine parts for the automotive and aviation industry. Below, Tim Schieber, a DWG Tech GmbH employee, talks about his job and daily activities on DWG Tech GmbH's English website.

R **1** **Read the text and answer the following questions in your own words.**

1. What do CNC machines do?
2. What problems can occur with CNC machines?

Hi, my name is Tim Schieber and I work as a CNC machine operator here at the DWG Tech headquarters in Stuttgart. I've been with the company since completing my apprenticeship three years ago and next summer I am going to work at the DWG Tech branch in Detroit.

In my opinion, what we do here is very important. CNC is all about precision, and it is therefore essential that I concentrate at all times. These machines drill, shape, cut and polish the parts for automobiles and aeroplanes. As a CNC machine operator I am responsible for one machine. As I said, this job is all about precision, and the machines are programmed specifically for each job. I do not do the programming myself, but I learnt programming during my apprenticeship and I sometimes have to intervene when something goes wrong – such as a vibrating workpiece or broken cutting tools.

The CNC process is almost entirely automatic. It is my job to set up the machine for the production process, which means loading the machine with the correct tools and workpieces. Once the programming for an operation is done, I enter the commands into the machine. To do this we use a computer network. The next step is to let the machine work its magic.

The main part of my job is to monitor the machine and spot problems. This means checking that the machine is running smoothly, measuring finished workpieces to check that the dimensions are correct, and sometimes replacing tools. It is also important that the machine is kept cool and lubricated with a special lubricating oil – but this is also done automatically. Of course, another of my tasks is to make sure the machine is kept clean, and that the working area is safe.

My working day depends on what shift I am on. We generally work either early shift or late shift. Early shift is from 6am until 2pm, and the guys on late shift begin at 2pm and clock out at 10pm. Sometimes, if we have a lot of work to do, there is also a night shift – but that doesn't happen too often. I actually prefer early shift. Even though I don't enjoy waking up at 4:45am, it is great to have the afternoon to do whatever I like – especially in the summer.

I really enjoy my job and I am proud to be working for an international company like DWG. My colleagues and I are always very busy and it can be fairly stressful. But I love working with the machines and it is interesting to see the many technological developments in the industry.

2 **Find the synonyms in the text for the following words:**

1. to finish
2. very important
3. cars
4. accuracy
5. to observe
6. usually
7. to like
8. workmates
9. quite

R **3** **Decide whether the statements are true or false. Give reasons for your decisions in German.**

1. Tim is currently doing an apprenticeship as a CNC machine operator.
2. Once the machine starts running, Tim's work is over.
3. One of Tim's tasks is making sure that the cutting tools are not broken.
4. Tim rarely works in shifts.
5. Accuracy is very important for CNC work.
6. The technology used in CNC machining has hardly changed over the years.

P **4** **Your boss has asked you to write a short text for your company's English website. Make sure you include some basic facts about your company and details about your daily tasks and responsibilities. Use some of the phrases in Tim's text, e.g. *I work as, I've been with the company since*, etc.**

→ **PHRASES:** Your company

P/I **5** **Check the Internet for a job in your industry that interests you. Make notes on the daily tasks and responsibilities.**

I **6** **Explain the job you researched to your partner, but don't mention the job title. Your partner must guess what the job is from the description you give. Then swap roles.**

C | Organisational structure

P/M KMK II **Sie sind Auszubildende(r) in der DWG Tech GmbH. Ihr Vorgesetzter benötigt eine Übersicht über die Ingenieursabteilung der DWG Tech GmbH Niederlassung in Detroit. Auf deren Firmen-Homepage finden Sie die folgenden Informationen zu den Mitarbeitern. Zeichnen Sie ein Organigramm nach der vorliegenden Beschreibung.**

Who's who in DWG Tech GmbH Detroit's engineering department?

DWG Tech GmbH Inc. employs around 60 people in its engineering department. The department is led by Chief Engineer Dr. Adam Foster, who is supported by his Personal Assistant Helen Green and DWG Tech's Assistant Chief Engineer Dr. Tim Bayliss. The engineering department is split into two core areas: automotive and aviation. Shift leaders Chris Falsone and Sandra Borowski report to Michael Kellermann, the foreman. They all belong to automotive which is run by experienced Chief Automotive Engineer, Dr. Torben Brinkema. DWG Tech's aviation department is in the capable hands of Dr. Judith Sommer, Chief Aviation Engineer, who has

been with the company for over 15 years. Dr. Sommer is supported by foreman Frank Kapowski. Barry Richardson and Jens Schmelzer are the two shift leaders and work closely with Mr Kapowski.

WORD BANK

aviation – Luftfahrt
CNC (computerized numerical control) – CNC (computerisierte numerische Steuerung)
dimensions – Maße
drill (v) – bohren
lubricated – geölt
lubricating oil – Schmieröl
measure (v) – messen
polish (v) – schleifen, polieren
precision – Genauigkeit
shape (v) – fräsen, formen
vibrate (v) – vibrieren
workpiece – Werkstück

WORD BANK ◎

braking system – Bremsanlage
cylinder head – Zylinderkopf
interface – Schnittstelle
manufacturing plant – Produktionsbetrieb
operating system – Betriebssystem

03

NACH DIESEM MODUL:

- ✓ kann ich auf Englisch die Verwendung verschiedener Transportsysteme erklären,
- ✓ kann ich auf Englisch die richtige Handhabung von Lasten erklären und Vorschriften zur Vermeidung von Verletzungen erläutern.

1

2

3

4

Moving goods in the warehouse

In the modern warehouse goods are often moved automatically using robots and conveyor belts. We can say that these handling systems are permanently installed because they are fixed in one place. Another way of moving goods is manually, where warehouse workers carry goods to their storage place. This is possible with goods that are light. Goods which are too heavy to be carried can be moved using mechanical handling equipment, such as forklift trucks or lifting carts.

1 Look at the photos of different types of handling systems. Say how the goods are moved in each photo.

2 Decide if the handling systems in the photos are permanently installed or more flexible. Write your answer in a table like the one below.

Permanently installed systems	Flexible systems

P **3** Say which of the handling systems in the photos are used at your place of work.

A | Automatic and mechanical handling systems

In a modern warehouse different handling systems are used to store and retrieve goods. The permanently installed systems are expensive to install but they are very efficient. Mechanical handling systems have other advantages; for example, this equipment is more flexible than permanently installed systems.

1 Look at the handling systems in the photos on page 24 again. Outline the advantages and disadvantages of each system. Use the phrases in the box.

		more money.
		safer.
	are	more reliably.
Permanently installed systems such as …	run	fewer workers.
Mechanical handling systems such as …	cost	flexible.
	need	inflexible.
		more workers.
		less money.

R **2** Mrs Schneider, the head storewoman of a warehouse in Hamburg is showing some visitors from Liverpool around. Listen to the dialogue and list the different kinds of handling systems that the speakers talk about.
A 3.18

R **3** Listen to the dialogue again and match the goods with the way they are handled.
A 3.18

Goods	How they are handled
1. books, paper 2. fashion items 3. hazardous goods	a. Goods are transported quickly and carefully. b. Goods of different sizes are moved on the ground and stacked on pallets. c. Goods are transported automatically between production areas. d. Goods have a solid, even surface and are moved automatically.

P **4** Think of five types of goods and choose the best way of handling them in the warehouse. Give reasons.

5 UNDERSTANDING TECHNICAL ENGLISH

1. Find the different meanings of the word 'handle' in an English-German dictionary.

2. Translate the sentences with 'handle' into German.
   a. It is important to handle hazardous goods carefully.
   b. If there is a problem, you have to handle the situation as best you can.
   c. Yesterday we had to handle 300 orders from our customers.
   d. The handle of the lifting cart broke so we could not use it.

WORD BANK

conveyor belt – Förderband
forklift (truck) – Gabelstapler
handling system – Handhabungssystem
hazardous – gefährlich
lifting cart – Hubwagen
mechanical handling equipment – mechanische Fördervorrichtungen
permanently installed (v) – fest installiert
retrieve (v) – wieder finden
stack (v) – stapeln
storage place – Lagerort, Lagerplatz
store (v) – (ein)lagern
warehouse process – Lagerprozess

WORD BANK ⊙

chemical warehouse – Lagerhaus für Chemikalien
fashion warehouse – Lagerhaus für Modeartikel
head storewoman – Lageristin
maneuver (v) – manövrieren
overhead conveyor system – Hängebahnanlage
pallet – Palette
pallet rack – Palettenregal
production area – Fertigungsbereich
roller conveyor – Rollenbahn

B | Manual handling regulations

Everyday tasks such as carrying heavy loads can lead to back and knee problems. Accidents which happen when handling hazardous goods can cause even more serious injuries. It is important to follow manual handling regulations and wear protective clothing to avoid long-term health problems.

1 **SAFETY FIRST**

Match the two parts of the manual handling regulations.

1. Bend your knees and try	a. close to your body.
2. Carry the load	b. to lift the load in a smooth motion.
3. Make sure that the object	c. is clear.
4. Keep your back	d. using a handling aid.
5. Heavy loads should be moved	e. straight when moving goods.
6. Make sure there is somewhere	f. to put the load down.
7. Check first if the route you want to take	g. is light enough to lift and stable enough to move.

P/I **2** **Tell your partner about the manual handling regulations you follow when moving goods in the warehouse. Use the phrases below.**

I try to carry the load …

Before I pick up goods, …

When I lift …, I make sure that …

When goods are heavy, …

3 **Complete the text about the risks in a warehouse using the words in the box.**

protective • repetitive • cost • injuries • risk • lifting • gases • forklifts

The risks of manual handling for warehouse workers

Warehouse workers who handle goods are at a greater **1** than someone who works in an office. Many of the **2** that happen in the warehouse involve manual handling. Warehouse workers often suffer with back problems from **3** loads that are too heavy. Even handling a light load can cause problems if the task is **4** or if it is carried out under bad conditions. Accidents can happen while driving **5** or when goods are not placed properly on racks and they fall onto workers. Warehouse workers who handle hazardous **6** may develop voice problems. Injured or sick workers **7** companies a lot of money every year. Something as simple as using a lifting cart to carry loads can reduce back problems. Workers who handle hazardous goods should always wear **8** clothing. It is not possible to prevent all accidents and injuries in the warehouse but we can reduce risks to a minimum.

C | Driving a forklift

R **1** KMK I

Sie erhalten demnächst eine Einweisung in das Fahren eines Gabelstaplers. Sie recherchieren im Internet und finden den folgenden englischen Text. Lesen Sie den Text und beantworten Sie die Fragen auf Deutsch.

1. Welche Aufgaben gehören zur Gabelstaplerfahrprüfung?
2. Was sollte man an den Reifen vor Inbetriebnahme des Gabelstaplers untersuchen?
3. Wonach müssen die Gabeln vor dem Fahren überprüft werden?

ww#.forklifttest.com

The forklift driving test includes starting the forklift, picking up a load and stacking it on top of something else.

- The driver must be able to drive backwards around turns and other obstacles.
- The driver must know when to use the horn and the lights.
- The driver must adjust the mirrors properly to see things behind the forklift.

Before using the forklift the driver has to check the following things:

- Are the tyres in good condition or do they have holes?
- Does the emergency brake work properly?
- If the forklift runs on batteries, does it have any loose connections?
- Can the forks pick up a load without any problems?
- Are the forks straight or not?
- Can the forks be moved up and down?
- Can they be moved to the left and the right?

M/I **2**

Sie haben in Ihrem Ausbildungsbetrieb einen englischen Praktikanten, der seine Gabelstablerprüfung bereits abgelegt hat. Ihr Ausbilder möchte ihm dazu einige Fragen stellen. Übernehmen Sie die Rolle des Dolmetschers für das Gespräch zwischen dem deutschen Ausbilder und dem englischen Praktikanten. Bilden Sie vollständige Fragen und Antworten mit Hilfe der Stichwörter.

Ausbilder	Dolmetscher	Englischer Praktikant
Fragen Sie, wie lange die Gabelstaplerausbildung gedauert hat. →	*basic training course / take* → ←	*five days*
Fragen Sie, ob es auch eine theoretische Prüfung in Großbritannien gibt. →	*written exam* → ←	*no written exam / certificate at the end*
Fragen Sie ihn, was beim Fahren eines Gabelstaplers aus Sicherheitsgründen am Wichtigsten ist. →	*safety reasons* → ←	*drive slowly*
Fragen Sie, ob es ihm Spaß macht einen Gabelstapler zu fahren. →	*enjoy* → ←	*yes / but not all day long*

WORD BANK

emergency brake – Notbremse
handling regulation – Handhabungsvorschrift
lift (v) – (hoch)heben
load – Last
pick up (v) – aufnehmen
protective clothing – Sicherheitskleidung

x3gj95

C

NACH DIESEM MODUL:

- √ kenne ich die wichtigsten Redewendungen um ein Telefongespräch zu führen,
- √ kann ich Maße, Namen und Adressen am Telefon auf Englisch weitergeben.

1

2

3

4

Telephoning

When you are on the job, chances are you will have your mobile phone with you – it does not matter what line of work you are in. Whether you are repairing a server, fixing a leak, or installing a telephone line, your phone can ring at any time. It could be a customer with a complaint, you may have to ring a supplier or check the status of an order. And if you have to talk in English, you need to have the necessary skills to understand and be understood, no matter what the situation.

P **1** **Look at the photos. What might the people be talking about on the telephone? Compare your answers with a partner. Use these words to help you:**

materials • problem • delay • support • help • breakdown • repair • solution • angry • confused • crash • computer network room

2 **Match the German words below with the English equivalents.**

1. Handy	a. message
2. Anrufbeantworter	b. hands-free device
3. Festnetz	c. extension number
4. Nachricht	d. mobile/cell phone
5. Durchwahl	e. answering machine
6. Freisprechanlage	f. area code
7. Vorwahl	g. country code
8. Ländervorwahl	h. landline

A | Making and receiving a phone call

R **1** **Which of the following phrases are used for making calls and which ones for receiving calls? Make a list.**

1. Could you put me through to Mr Warren, please?
2. I'm sorry, but Mr/Ms … is in a meeting at the moment.
3. How can I help you?
4. Thank you. I'll ring back later.
5. Can I ask what your call is about?
6. Would you like to leave a message?
7. Thank you very much for your help.
8. My name is Barry Potter and I'm calling from …
9. May I take your name, please?
10. I'd like to speak to somebody in the production department, please.
11. Hold the line, please. I'll put you through.
12. Could you tell him/her that …?

M **2** **Read the telephone conversation below and find the English equivalents for the following German expressions.**

→ **PHRASES:** Telephoning

1. Haben Sie etwas zum Schreiben?
2. Soll ich Ihnen seine Handynummer geben?
3. Er ist leider zurzeit nicht im Büro.
4. Ich hätte gerne mit … gesprochen.
5. Einen Moment, bitte.
6. Wie kann ich Ihnen helfen?

Christoph:	Smart EDV, Christoph Fink.
Caller:	Er, yes, hello. Do you speak English?
Christoph:	Certainly. How can I help you?
Caller:	This is the Smart IT company in Kiel, isn't it?
Christoph:	Yes, that's correct.
Caller:	Great. My name is Erik Pedersen and I'm calling from Danske Onlinebank Copenhagen. I'd like to speak to Mr Gebhardt, please.
Christoph:	Sorry, but Mr Gebhardt is not in the office at the moment. Can I take a message, or would you like his mobile number?
Caller:	Can you give me his mobile number, please?
Christoph:	Ok, do you have a pen?
Caller:	Just a second, please … ok, go ahead.
Christoph:	The number is 0049-170 557624.
Caller:	Sorry, I didn't catch that. Could you speak up a bit?
Christoph:	Yes, of course. The number is 0049-170 557624.
Caller:	Thank you very much.
Christoph:	You're welcome. Maybe you can give me your phone number.
Caller:	Certainly. It's 0045, that's the country code for Denmark, 32, the area code for Copenhagen, and then 54 58 11. Oh, and my extension number is 944.
Christoph:	0045-32 54 58 11, extension 944. Thank you very much. Goodbye.
Caller:	Goodbye.

WORD BANK

breakdown – Störung, Ausfall
crash – Absturz
leak – Leck

INTERCULTURAL BOX

Intercultural awareness – Telephoning in English-speaking countries

When talking on the phone in English it is important that you use suitable and polite phrases. For example, if you know the person you are calling, it is common to make a little small talk before getting down to business. One thing to remember: Although it is common for English people to quickly switch to first names, it is still important to remain polite and remember that you are talking to a customer or a colleague, and not your best friend.
Example: *How are you? I haven't spoken to you for a while.*
If you have to give bad news or talk about a problem, then you should begin with *I'm afraid …* or *Unfortunately … .*
Example: *I'm afraid we cannot install your wireless internet connection this week.*
A request often begins with *Could you possibly …* or *I would be grateful if you would / could … .*
Example: *I would be grateful if you would call me back later.*
When someone thanks you for your help, or for a job well done, you can simply say *You're welcome.* And be careful! Whereas in German, just saying *yes* or *no* may be fine, this is considered to be quite impolite in England. Instead, just say *Yes, I think so*, or *No, I'm afraid not.* If you call somebody, you should give your name, where you are calling from, and say who you would like to speak to.
Example: *Hello, my name is Felix Hirschbach, calling from Crown Electronics. Could I speak to Ms Cameron, please?*

P **3** **How would you say the following things more politely?**

→ **PHRASES:** Telephoning

1. Eh? Say it again!
2. Give me your number!
3. What do you want?
4. What's your name?
5. I can't hear you!
6. What?
7. He's not here!
8. Give me Ms Bauer!

I **4** KMK I **Sie arbeiten im International Calls Service Center von Smart EDV in Kiel und erhalten einen Anruf. Führen Sie das folgende Telefongespräch mit einem Partner auf Englisch.**

Smart EDV GmbH, Kiel.	Stefanie Berg, dänische Kundin
Nehmen Sie den Anruf entgegen.	→ Nennen Sie Ihren Namen. Sie möchten mit Herrn Gebhardt sprechen.
Sagen Sie, dass Sie die Anruferin schlecht verstehen und bitten Sie sie, etwas lauter zu sprechen.	Sprechen Sie etwas lauter und fragen Sie, ob Sie jetzt besser zu verstehen sind.
Bejahen Sie und fragen Sie, worum es geht.	Erklären Sie, dass die Firma Smart EDV gestern in Ihrer Firma neue Hardware und Software installiert hat, und dass heute Morgen der Server abgestürzt ist. Es ist dringend!
Sagen Sie höflich, dass Herr Gebhardt in einer Sitzung ist und sich später melden wird. Fragen Sie, ob Herr Gebhardt die Nummer der Anruferin hat.	Bejahen Sie. Bedanken Sie sich und beenden Sie das Gespräch.
Bedanken Sie sich auch und verabschieden Sie sich.	

B | Giving information over the phone

Making a quick call is often the fastest and easiest way of passing on valuable information, such as measurements or figures. However, misunderstandings can happen very quickly, so it is important to make sure any information is delivered clearly and correctly.

1 Match the English word to the German translation.

1. height	a. Breite
2. length	b. Gewicht
3. width	c. Höhe
4. weight	d. Tiefe
5. depth	e. Länge

INFO BOX: Saying weights and measurements

nine **point** five milimetres (9.5 mm)	100 **by** 30 **by** 15 (100 x 30 x 15)
thirty one **square** metres (31 m²)	twenty **cubic** metres (20 m³)
one **point** two five litre engine (1.25 l)	6000 revolutions **per** minute (6000 rpm)
170 kilometers **per** hour (170 kph)	two hundred **and** twenty volts (220 V)

2 What are the adjectives for the nouns in exercise 1?

I **3** Sit back to back with a partner. Take turns in giving each other different information over the phone. Partner A uses role card A, Partner B uses role card B (see Appendix).

I **4** Sit back to back and spell your name, the name and address of your company, and your email address. Use the table below to help you.

Symbol	Name	Example
@	at	info@
B / b	capital letter / lower case	NYC / asap
-	hyphen / dash	t-online
ö	o-umlaut / oe / o with two dots	Schönberg
:	colon	http:
/	slash / stroke / forward slash	org/news
\	backslash	\docs
.	dot	.de
_	underscore	customer_info

R **5** KMK I ◎ A 1.3 Alex Bauder works for Fertighaus Henke in Magdeburg and is called by Mr. Reid, an English customer who lives in Germany and who is currently building a house near Magdeburg. Listen to the conversation and answer the following questions in German.

1. Who is Mr Deschler?
2. Why can't Mr Reid speak to him personally?
3. Why does Mr Reid want to speak to Mr Deschler?
4. When will Fertighaus Henke begin building Mr Reid's cellar?
5. Why does the extractor fan need to be moved to the left?
6. Which changes is Mr Deschler not responsible for?
7. What should Mr Deschler do next?

R **6** ◎ A 1.3 Now listen to the conversation again and make notes of the changes Mr Reid wants, where he wants them, and details about the measurements, where given.

WORD BANK

cubic metre – Kubikmeter
revolutions per minute – Drehzahl
socket – Steckdose
square metre – Quadratmeter

WORD BANK ◎

construction manager – Bauleiter
diameter – Durchmesser
extractor fan – Dunstabzugshaube
foundation pit – Baugrube
hob – Kochfeld

04

NACH DIESEM MODUL:

- ✓ kann ich auf Englisch verschiedene Kommissioniersysteme und Auslagerungsprinzipien erklären,
- ✓ kann ich auf Englisch erläutern, welche Kriterien bei der Wahl der Kommissioniermethode wichtig sind.

Picking and consigning goods

After an order is placed by the customer, the goods have to be picked in the warehouse before they can be packed and shipped. Order picking and consigning must be done carefully because they directly influence customer satisfaction.

1 Look at the picture and describe what the workers are doing to complete a customer's order. Use the words in the box.

lifting cart • to load up • pallet racks • picking list • storage place

2 Partner A uses the picking list below and partner B uses the picking list on page 84. Ask your partner for the missing information and complete your picking list.

Partner A

Sold to: Weidner KG Am Feld 31, 38100 Braunschweig	**Salesperson no.:** 3 **Order no.:** 123
Ship to: 1	**Date shipped:** 4
Item no.: 315346	**Quantity ordered:** 200; **shipped:** 5
Description: 2	**Terms:** DDP (delivered duty paid)
Account no.: 3429168	**Storage area:** 6

A | Order picking systems

There are two main order picking systems: the picker-to-part system and the part-to-picker system.

R **1** ⓪A 3.19 **Listen to the conversation, in which order picker Frank Brown is explaining the two picking systems to Susan Kelly, a new warehouse worker. Decide whether the following statements are true or false. Then correct the false statements.**

1. Both picking systems require a storage area, a picking area and a material handling system.
2. Order pickers are always informed via headset about which items to pick.
3. In the picker-to-part system the goods automatically arrive at the picking bay.
4. At each bay the picking operator receives the items for only one order.
5. The part-to-picker system is mainly used in smaller warehouses.

2 **Look at some of the advantages and disadvantages of each order picking system and put them in the table below.**

- long/no search times
- some/no lost time while waiting for articles from the storage places
- high/low capital expenditure
- short/long picking time for articles

Picker-to-part system	Part-to-picker system
– long search times	– no search times

3 **Compare your results in exercise 2 with your partner. Add more advantages and disadvantages to your tables.**

P **4** **Which order picking system is used at your place of work? Report to the class.**

B | Order picking methods

Optimising the picking process is important because order picking is a labour-intensive and expensive activity. The cost of order picking can be as much as 50% of total warehouse expenses. Three picking methods are widely used: sequential order picking, parallel order picking and parallel sequential picking.

R **1** **Read the descriptions of the different order picking methods on page 34 and match them to the correct diagrams.**

WORD BANK

consign (v) – versenden
customer's order – Kundenauftrag
lifting cart – Hubwagen
order picker – Kommissionierer(in)
order picking – Kommissionieren, Auftragszusammenstellung
pallet rack – Palettenregal
parallel order picking – auftragsorientierte, parallele Kommissionierung
parallel sequential order picking – serienorientierte, parallele Kommissionierung
pick (v) – kommissionieren, entnehmen
picking list – Kommissionierliste
sequential order picking – autragsorientierte, serielle Kommissionierung
storage place – Lagerort

WORD BANK ⓪

dispatch – Versand
material handling system – Transportanlage
picking area – Kommissionier-bereich
picking bay – Kommissionierplatz

Parallel sequential order picking
This means that an order is completed for more than one customer at the same time. Several orders are combined into a series. The series is then divided into sub-series to complete the order simultaneously in different warehouse zones. In the end the sub-series are combined and sorted by orders.

Parallel order picking
Here an order is completed for one customer at a time. The order is divided into partial orders. Various order pickers work simultaneously on the same order in different picking zones. Later the partial orders are put together to complete the order for the customer.

Sequential order picking
In this process the order for only one customer is completed and one order picker deals with the order until it is completed. The order picker visits different picking zones, picks the ordered goods and completes the order.

Order picking method 1

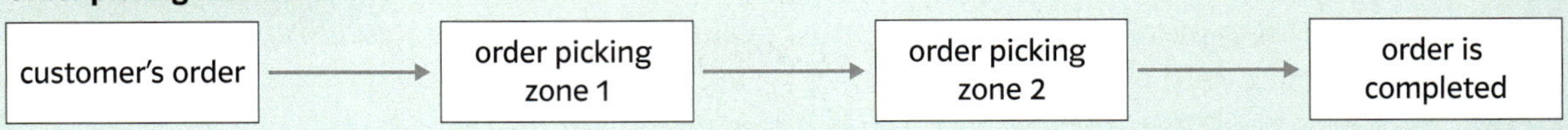

Order picking method 2

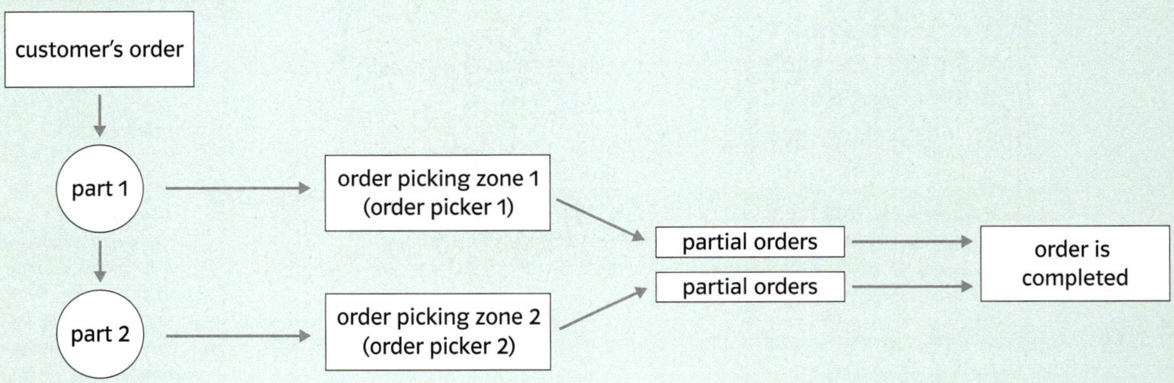

Order picking method 3

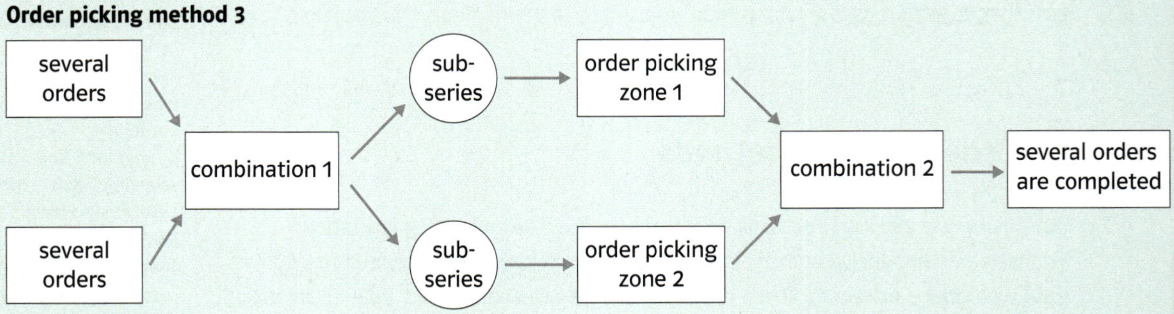

P **2** Use the diagrams above to explain the different order picking methods to each other.

P **3** Which order picking method is best for which warehouse? Discuss the advantages and disadvantages of each picking method and present your results to the class.

→ **PHRASES:** Presentations

4 **UNDERSTANDING TECHNICAL ENGLISH**

Make a list of the tasks at your workplace that are done 'parallel', 'sequentially' or 'parallel sequentially'. Report to the class.

M KMK II 5 **Bei der Auftragsbearbeitung stellt die Kommissionierzeit einen beachtlichen Zeit- und Kostenfaktor dar. Sie finden in einer amerikanischen Fachzeitschrift die folgenden Optimierungsvorschläge. Fassen Sie für die nächste Teambesprechung die Faktoren, die Einfluss auf die Effizienz haben, sowie die vier Phasen, die optimiert werden können, auf Deutsch zusammen.**

How to optimize picking times

Order picking is one of the most important activities in a warehouse. It is necessary to constantly improve its efficiency because the picking process contributes significantly to the warehouse operating costs. Main factors influencing the efficiency of order picking include product demand, warehouse layout, location of the items and picking method in combination with routing methods.

In order to improve the picking process, different measurements may help to optimize picking times. The processes for which time measurements are useful can be divided into four phases. The first phase is the time the picker needs to reach the picking point. The second phase is the time needed to find the products. The third phase is the time needed to collect the products from where they are stored. Phase four is the time the picker needs to transport the goods to the order point.

C | Storage systems

The storage system determines how long goods are stored and when they are picked from their storage places. The main storage systems are FIFO, LIFO, HIFO and LOFO.

1 **Match the storage systems to their meanings.**

1. FIFO	a. highest (in price) in, first out
2. HIFO	b. first in, first out
3. LIFO	c. lowest (in price) in, first out
4. LOFO	d. last in, first out

P 2 **Discuss with your partner which storage system is best for perishables. Give reasons.**

P 3 **Write a short report about the storage system used at your place of work.**

WORD BANK

efficiency – Effizienz
operating costs – laufende Kosten
partial order – Teilauftrag
perishables – (leicht) verderbliche Ware(n)
routing method – elektronisches System zur Übermittlung von Aufträgen
storage system – Lagersystem
store (v) – (ein)lagern
sub-series – Unterserie(n)

D

NACH DIESEM MODUL:

- ✓ kann ich auf Englisch kurze Anfragen, Angebote und Bestellungen als Brief, E-Mail oder Fax erstellen,
- ✓ kann ich englische Briefe, E-Mails und Faxe beantworten.

1

2

3

4

Written communication

Written communication such as emails, faxes and business letters play an essential role in business, both in the office and the workshop. For any company to run efficiently, it is necessary to have an effective communication system – making sure that enquiries are answered promptly, offers are made on time, and orders are placed and processed correctly. The standard business letter has been replaced in recent years by the faster email, and to a lesser extent, the fax. In all areas of business today it is common to have dealings with countries across the globe, meaning you need to be able to understand written communication in English.

P **1** **Look at the pictures above and describe them in your own words.**

P **2** **What are the advantages and disadvantages of the forms of written communication shown in the pictures? Create a list. Use these words to help you:**

confidential • instant • easy • time-consuming • reliable • signal • misunderstanding • slow • personal • formal • informal

3 **Compare your lists with a partner and come up with a final list for each form of communication. Share your final list with the class.**

A | Enquiries

Business transactions generally begin with an enquiry. In the example below, a car garage is looking for a new supplier of tools.

M **1** **Stephen Bains from City Garage in Wolverhampton, England is interested in buying some tools from Hauch Werkzeuge KG in Gelsenkirchen, a toolmaking company specializing in tools for car mechanics. Read Stephen's enquiry and sum up the main information in German.**

Dear Sir/Madam,	a. appropriate salutation
Automotive mechanic tool supplier	b. subject line
We saw your advertisement in this month's edition of *Under the Bonnet* magazine regarding your selection of tools for car mechanics.	c. source of address
We are a family-run car mechanic company in Wolverhampton, England, with over 20 employees.	d. introduction of your firm
We have recently expanded and are looking for a new supplier of quality tools for our new workshops. Therefore we would ask you to send us a copy of your latest catalogue and price list.	e. reason for enquiry f. request to send catalogue and price list
Please also inform us about your export prices and possible discounts as well as terms of payment and delivery and delivery times.	g. request for information on prices and discounts and terms of payment and delivery
As we would like to test your tools, we would appreciate it if you could send us some samples.	h. further requests
Thank you for your attention to this enquiry and we look forward to hearing from you.	i. closing phrase
Yours sincerely,	j. complimentary close

R **2** **Match these parts of an enquiry with the descriptions (a.–j.) above.**

1. Best wishes.
2. Your company was recommended to me by a colleague.
3. We are a large production company, specialising in machine components.
4. Please let us have a detailed cost estimate for configuring our IT network.
5. We hope to hear from you soon.
6. What are your terms of payment for regular customers?
7. As we are convinced that your products will sell well on the American market …
8. A visit by your representative would be greatly appreciated.
9. Please let us know whether you can supply from stock.
10. Machine component supplier

WORD BANK

bonnet – Motorhaube
car mechanic – KFZ-Mechaniker(in)
toolmaking company – Werkzeugmacher
workshop – Werkstatt

B | Offers

P **1** **Read the offer email below and complete it using the words from the box.**

bank transfer • discount • interest • business • working days • sample • attachment • delivery period • stock • orders

From: mailto:t.wolf@hauch...de **Sent:** 201_-05-30 14:52
To: mailto:info@citygarage.co...uk
Cc: mailto:k.mueller@hauch...de
Subject: Your enquiry

Attachments Hauptkatalog_2012.pdf

Dear Mr Bains

Thank you for your enquiry and your **1** in our products.

We are sending you our latest brochure and price list as an **2**.
For **3** of 200 units or more we are able to grant a quantity **4** of five per cent.
For large orders (over 250 units) we require a **5** of 10–14 **6**.
Smaller orders can be delivered from **7** and within 3–5 working days.

Our usual terms of payment are by **8** to our account with the GDB Bank in Gelsenkirchen.

One **9** case of ratchets, sockets, wrenches and screwdrivers has been dispatched to you this morning and should reach you in the next few days.

Thank you again for your enquiry. We look forward to establishing regular **10** with you.

Yours sincerely

Tim Wolf

P **2** **Use the following notes to write an enquiry and an offer in English.**

→ **PHRASES:** Written communication

Enquiry
(You work at Construct World.)

- large DIY store in Poland (Construct World), looking to buy quality German-made tools
- saw your company (Hauch Werkzeuge KG) at a trade show in Hannover
- would like information about delivery times, discounts, copy of catalogue
- would like some samples to inspect
- polite ending

Angebot
(Sie arbeiten bei Hauch Werkzeuge.)

- Bedanken Sie sich für die Anfrage.
- Gerne schicken Sie Ihren aktuellen Prospekt inklusive Preisliste zu.
- Lieferzeit (nach Polen): große Bestellungen (über 500 Stück): 5–10 Werktage, kleine Bestellungen: 2–4 Werktage
- Preisnachlass ab Bestellwert von 2.500 € möglich (5 %)
- Sie würden sich freuen, mit Construct World zusammenarbeiten zu dürfen.
- höflicher Schluss

C | Orders

1 **Read the order fax below and complete it using the prepositions in the box below.**

for (2x) • by • of • to (3x) • with

TELEFAX Message

City Garage
17 Gorsebrook Rd.
Wolverhampton WV6 5PI
Tel.: 0044 (0)1902 554997... • Fax: 0044 (0)1902 554998...

To: Hauch Werkzeuge KG
Schmiedstrasse 44
45879 Gelsenkirchen
Germany

Attention: Mr Tim Wolf

Fax: 0049 209 721965...

From: Stephen Bains

Subject: Order

Dear Mr Wolf

Thank you very much **1** your email **2** 30 May.

Thank you also for sending us your catalogue and price list.
We were very impressed **3** your range of tools for car mechanics and would like to place a trial order **4** 16 socket sets, 16 screwdriver sets, 30 adjustable wrenches and 16 torque wrenches.

Please confirm this order indicating the bank account **5** which you wish to have the sum in question transferred.

Please deliver the tools **6** our workshop at 17 Gorsebrook Rd., Wolverhampton, WV6 5PI.

We look forward **7** receiving the consignment soon and to placing further orders **8** you.

Best regards

S.Bains

Stephen Bains

M **2** KMK II **Sie arbeiten bei Hauch Werkzeuge KG in Gelsenkirchen. Ihr Chef bittet Sie, das obige Fax für ihn auf Deutsch zusammenzufassen, damit er über den Auftrag informiert ist.**

WORD BANK

ratchet – Knarre
screwdriver – Schraubenzieher / -dreher
socket – Steckdose, Stecknuss
torque wrench – Drehmoment-schlüssel
(adjustable) wrench – (verstellbarer) Schraubenschlüssel

05

NACH DIESEM MODUL:

- ✓ kann ich Verpackungsarten und deren Verwendung auf Englisch erklären,
- ✓ kann ich auf Englisch geeignete Packhilfsmittel nennen und erläutern,
- ✓ kann ich auf Englisch Handhabungssymbole erklären und auf Risiken beim Verladen von Waren hinweisen.

Packing goods

Up until the early twentieth century most products didn't need to be packed. However, today products are sent to all parts of the world and need adequate packing for transport and storage. The most important purpose of packing is, therefore, to make sure that the goods reach the customer safely and undamaged.

1 Look at the pictures and match them with the correct captions.

1. Stocking goods in wooden crates
2. Different handling symbols on a cardboard box
3. A stack of freight containers at the docks
4. Stacked wood held together by straps

2 The cardboard box in picture 4 is labelled with various signs. Explain them by completing the following sentences with the words in the box.

keep products dry • handle with care • this side up

a. The sign with the glass means: ? .
b. The two arrows tell you that you should transport the box ? .
c. The umbrella means that you must ? .

A | Adequate packaging

The right form of packaging needs to be chosen for each product to protect the goods during transport and storage.

1 Look at the English terms for different types of packaging and match them to the photos. Use the word bank for help if necessary.

bale • barrel • crate • drum • pallet • sack

R **2** Florian Steinbach is a German intern at a warehouse in the USA. Listen to his conversation with the packer Sean Miles and complete the table.
◎ A 3.20

Protection against	Transport	Storage
– humidity	– …	– …

P **3** ⚠ Add at least two more points to each column in exercise 2.

P/I **4** Discuss the advantages and disadvantages of different types of packaging. Take notes and compare your findings in class.

WATCH OUT!
Der Begriff _packing_ bezeichnet den „Prozess des Verpackens", während sich _packaging_ auf das „Verpackungsmaterial" bezieht. In der Praxis werden beide Begriffe jedoch oft synonym als Bezeichnung für „Verpackung" verwendet.

I **5** KMK II Während Ihrer Ausbildung haben Sie sechs Wochen in einer Firma in London verbracht. Vor Ihrer Abreise haben Sie noch ein Abschlussgespräch mit dem/der dortigen Lagerleiter(in). Führen das Gespräch mit Hilfe der Rollenkarten auf S. 84 und S. 85. Tauschen Sie anschließend die Rollen.

WORD BANK

bale – Ballen
barrel – Fass, Tonne
cardboard box – Pappkarton
crate – Kiste
dock – Dock, Kai, Hafenbecken
drum – Trommel, Behälter
freight container – Frachtcontainer
handling symbol – Handhabungssymbol
label (v) – etikettieren, kennzeichnen, beschriften
pallet – Palette
packaging – Verpackung(smaterial)
packing – Verpacken, Verpackung
protect (v) – schützen
stack – Stapel
stock (v) – (ein)lagern
storage – Lager(haltung)
strap – Band, Riemen

WORD BANK ◎

drop (v) – fallen lassen
fragile – zerbrechlich
humidity – Feuchtigkeit

B | Packing materials

Packing materials, such as bubble wrap or foam peanuts, protect goods from humidity, pressure or being dropped and broken.

1 Look at the photos and match the packing materials with the correct names. Give examples of goods that could be packed with them.

adhesive tape • bubble wrap • foam peanuts • packing paper • polystyrene • rope

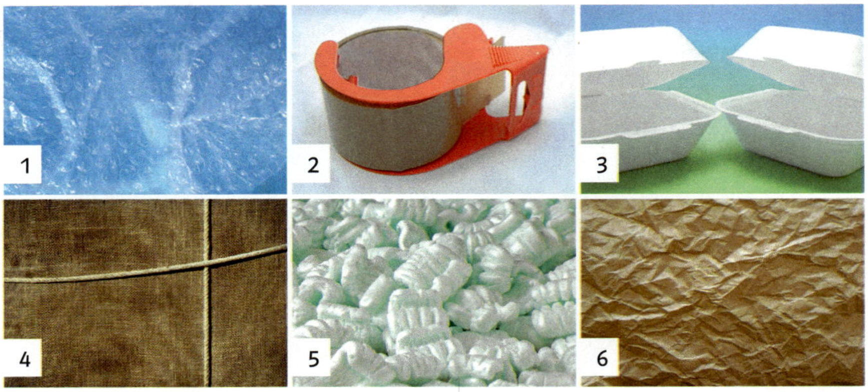

R **2** Read the text and answer the questions.

1. Which packing materials can be used for cushioning goods? Bubble wrap
2. How can you fill empty space? packing paper, foam peanuts
3. Which material should not be used to fill empty space? Why? newspaper
4. With the help of which packing materials can you fix goods during transport? rope.

http://ww#.10minutetutorials.net

Different types of packing materials

Adhesive tape is often used to close boxes firmly. Make sure you use a strong and wide plastic tape. For good cushioning you can use bubble wrap, which you can cut to almost any size. Several layers should be used to make sure that the product is well protected. Don't forget corners and edges!
To fill empty space inside a package you can use packing paper. Don't use newspaper because the print may come off. Nowadays foam peanuts are often used, too. They easily fill empty spaces around lightweight and non-fragile items. Use enough foam peanuts so that the goods don't move when you shake the box.
With the help of different coloured stickers you can label each box according to the way the item should be handled.
Last but not least, ropes and bungee cords should be used to secure large items during transportation.

P **3** Which packing materials do you use at your company? What products are they used for and why?

4 UNDERSTANDING TECHNICAL ENGLISH
Look up the words 'packing' and 'packaging' in a dictionary and write three sentences with each term.

C | Handling signs

It is very important that goods are labelled to make sure that they are handled correctly during storage, loading and transportation.

1 Look at the handling signs and match them with the correct meanings.

don't use hooks • centre of gravity • don't stack • don't use blades •
no handtruck here • temperature limitation

R/P **2** Search the Internet for products that should be labelled with one or more of the handling signs in exercise 1.

D | Loading goods

When loading goods certain safety rules help to make sure that the workers stay healthy and the goods don't get damaged.

M **1** Read the text excerpt and summarize the main points in German.

> Risks are often underestimated when loading goods onto different means of transport. Loading docks are sometimes dirty and slippery. In many cases, the stairs along the loading dock are not used or fall protection is missing. Sometimes truck drivers forget to secure their trucks against rolling away while goods are being loaded. Wrong manoeuvring at the loading ramp can be avoided by making sure that drivers are given clear instructions.

2 SAFETY FIRST ⚠
Look at the Dos and Don'ts when loading and securing goods on a truck. Correct the false statements.

1. Make sure the vehicle load space is right for the type and size of the load.
2. Use the correct loading dock for your truck.
3. Overload your vehicle.
4. Don't use too many lashings to secure your load.
5. Make sure that loads cannot fall off your truck.
6. Forget to check your load before leaving the loading dock.
7. Take risks when transporting your load.

P **3** Prepare a short report about safety rules at your workplace.

WORD BANK

adhesive tape – Klebeband
blade – Klinge
bubble wrap – Luftpolsterfolie
bungee cord – Gummiband
cushioning – Polsterung
fall protection – Absturzsicherung
fix (v) – befestigen, fixieren
foam peanut – Schaumstofferdnuss
fork-lift truck – Gabelstapler
handtruck – Steckkarre
hook – Haken
lashing – Verschnürung
load space – Ladefläche
loading dock – Laderampe
overload (v) – überladen
packing paper – Packpapier
polystyrene – Styropor
rope – Band, Seil
safety rule – Sicherheitsvorschrift
secure (v) – (ab)sichern, schützen

5zw8jx

E

NACH DIESEM MODUL:

- ✓ kann ich eine Stellenanzeige auf Englisch verstehen,
- ✓ kann ich meine Fähigkeiten und Qualifikationen auf Englisch beschreiben,
- ✓ kann ich eine Bewerbung auf Englisch schreiben.

1

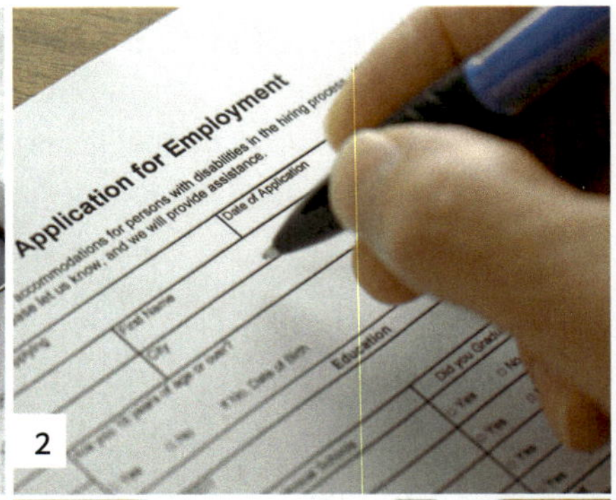

2

3

4

Applications

The world today is full of opportunities. You might decide to work in your hometown, a big city, or even another country. Maybe you want to work for a small family-run company or a major corporation with branches across the globe. Whatever you decide, the opportunities are out there, but it is up to you to take them.

1 **Look at the pictures above and describe them using the words below.**

> to apply • job advertisement • letter of application • CV • to search • job interview • employment contract • to invite • newspaper • to write

2 **Put the steps of the application process shown in the pictures above into the correct order.**

P **3** **Work on your own. What skills and qualifications do you need for a job in your industry? Make a list. Use these words to help you:**

> hard-working • motivated • logical • good with numbers • good with your hands • communicative • good team player • technical skills • able to understand plans and diagrams • attention to detail • computer skills

4 **Work with a partner and decide upon a final list. Share it with the class.**

A | Job advertisements

M/R **1** **Read the three online job advertisements below and find the English translations for the following German words and expressions.**

1. verantwortungsbewusst
2. aktiv, praktisch
3. Bewerber
4. Störungssuche
5. pünktlich
6. lernbereit
7. begeistert
8. gültige Fahrerlaubnis
9. Erfahrung
10. abgeschlossene Ausbildung
11. gute Bezahlung
12. fließendes Englisch
13. teamfähig
14. Montage
15. Grundkenntnisse in CAD
16. freie Stelle

ww#.totaljobs.com

1	City Garage – Car mechanic (full-time)	City Garage in Wolverhampton is looking for a recently-qualified car mechanic to join our busy team. Are you enthusiastic, willing to learn, responsible and punctual? If so, then contact us. We offer good rates of pay and a pleasant working atmosphere. Applicants must have a clean and valid driver's license. Please send a written application and a CV to Michael McCarthy at the following address: City Garage 17 Gorsebrook Rd. Wolverhampton WV6 5PI Tel.: 0044 (0)1902 554997...
2	Harper Shipping Client Support Technician	We are looking for a client support technician for our IT team to provide support and troubleshooting for hardware and software installation. You will also be responsible for new system configuration and maintaining the desktop client software. You should have two years experience, good English skills and be able to work as part of a team. Salary: negotiable Email application to: careers@HS...com
3	Trafford Tools Mechatronic Technician	Trafford Tools is a leading supplier of high-quality tools. We have a vacancy for a hands-on person to work as a mechatronic technician. Tasks: fault finding, maintenance, assembly, assist with installation. Skills: completed apprenticeship, basic CAD skills, good knowledge of tools, fluent English. Contact: James Truman J.truman@TT...co.uk Tel: 0044 (0)161 929496...

I/M **2** **One of your colleagues does not speak English and asks you to tell him about one of the job ads. Choose one of the ads and give him a brief summary in German. Swap roles.**

WORD BANK

branch – Filiale
family-run company – Familienunternehmen
job application – Bewerbung
maintain (v) – warten
opportunities – Möglichkeiten
qualifications – Qualifikationen
skills – Fähigkeiten
troubleshooting – Fehlerbehebung

B | Letter of application

R **1** **Read the letter of application and decide whether the following statements are true or false. Give reasons for your decisions.**

1. Erkan is in the final year of his apprenticeship as a car mechanic.
2. He has always wanted to be a car mechanic.
3. Erkan had a holiday job at *Werkstatt Kuhn.*
4. He is looking forward to working abroad.
5. Erkan has included his CV in the application.

Erkan Celik • Waldstrasse 48 • 50679 Köln • Germany

Michael McCarthy
City Garage
17 Gorsebrook Rd.
Wolverhampton
WV6 5PI
England

12 June 20_

Dear Mr McCarthy,

Application for job as car mechanic

I am writing to apply for the advertised position of a car mechanic at City Garage. I completed my apprenticeship as a car mechanic at a technical college here in Germany six months ago. I have been interested in cars since I was a child and being a car mechanic is my dream job.
As you will see from my CV, I recently completed a six-month internship at Werskstatt Kuhn. This not only gave me the opportunity to put my theoretical skills into practice, but I also had the chance to gain more experience with customers.
I am a very enthusiastic person. I am also reliable, responsible and willing to learn. Furthermore, I have good English skills and I would welcome the opportunity to gain some experience working in another country.
Thank you in advance for considering my application. If you require any further information, please contact me.

Yours sincerely,
Erkan Celik

Encl.: CV

WATCH OUT!
I am interested ~~for~~ cars. I am interested <u>in</u> cars.

M **2** **Fassen Sie mit Hilfe der unten stehenden Stichworte die wichtigsten Inhalte des Bewerbungsschreibens auf Deutsch zusammen.**
KMK I

1. Beruf, für den sich Erkan bewirbt 2. Berufserfahrung 3. Motivation
4. Persönliche Qualifikationen/Fähigkeiten 5. Kontaktperson

C | The CV

R **1** KMK II ⓞ A 1.4 **Andrea Wagner ist Auszubildende bei einer IT-Firma in Nürnberg. Sie möchte sich für eine Praktikumsstelle in der englischen Niederlassung ihrer Firma bewerben und fragt David, einen Praktikanten aus England, ob er ihr ein paar Tipps geben kann. Hören Sie das Gespräch an und vervollständigen Sie die folgenden Sätze auf Deutsch.**

1. Andrea möchte sich für eine Praktikumsstelle in ? bewerben.
2. Sie bringt am Montag ? mit ins Büro.
3. Der Lebenslauf sollte nicht länger sein als ? .
4. Man sollte niemals einen Lebenslauf ohne ? senden.
5. Man sollte den Lebenslauf dazu benutzen, seine ? und ? hervorzuheben.
6. Wenn man seine Arbeitserfahrung auflistet, sollte man mit ? anfangen.
7. In England muss ein Lebenslauf kein ? enthalten.
8 Man sollte sicherstellen, dass man zwei ? nennt.
9. Man sollte niemals ? .
10. Wenn der Lebenslauf fertig ist, sollte man ihn auf ? und ? überprüfen.
11. Es ist eine gute Idee, den Lebenslauf ? zu geben.
12. Wenn man den Lebenslauf abschickt, sollte man ? behalten.

P **2** KMK II **Verfassen Sie ein Anschreiben für eine der in Modulteil A ausgeschriebenen Stellen auf Englisch. Arbeiten Sie dabei die unten aufgeführten Inhalte ein.**

→ **PHRASES:** Applications

- Wählen Sie einen geeigneten Betreff.
- Nehmen Sie Bezug auf die Stellenanzeige und bekunden Sie Ihr Interesse an der ausgeschriebenen Stelle.
- Sie werden bald Ihre Ausbildung als … abschließen.
- Bringen Sie zum Ausdruck, dass Sie ein geeigneter Bewerber sind: organisiert, erfahren, hoch motiviert, teamfähig, flexibel, lernbereit, zuverlässig. Sie haben gute Englischkenntnisse.
- Beenden Sie den Brief angemessen und unterschreiben Sie.
- Weisen Sie auf Ihren Lebenslauf hin.

WORD BANK

consider (v) – betrachten
gain (v) – sammeln
internship – Praktikum
letter of application – Bewerbungsschreiben
reliable – zuverlässig
require (v) – benötigen

INFO BOX: Translating German school types and qualifications

It is not always possible to find the equivalent of your school type or qualification in English. However, the following table gives some useful translations.

Schools			
Grundschule	Elementary school / Primary school	Berufsschule (Duales System)	Part-time vocational school (dual system)
Hauptschule	General secondary school	Berufsfachschule	Full-time vocational school
Realschule	Intermediate secondary school	Fachschule für technische Berufe	Technical college
Gymnasium	Upper secondary school	Fachoberschule	Upper secondary vocational school
Gesamtschule	Comprehensive school	Fachgymnasium	Specialized upper secondary school

Qualifications			
Hauptschulabschluss	secondary modern school qualification	Fachabitur	advanced vocational certificate of education
Mittlere Reife	secondary school leaving certificate	Zusatzqualifikation	additional qualification
Abitur	A level/high school diploma		

06

NACH DIESEM MODUL:

- ✓ kann ich auf Englisch Sicherheitsvorkehrungen und Richtlinien im Umgang mit Gefahrengut nennen,
- ✓ kann ich auf Englisch die Bedeutung von Warnschildern erläutern.

1

2

Handling dangerous goods

Dangerous goods usually refer to solids, gases or liquids which might be a danger to health, property, equipment and the environment. People who handle hazardous goods must therefore wear protective clothing and follow safety precautions. It is also important to use the right packaging and to load hazardous goods securely.

1 Match the words for protective clothing with their German equivalents.

1. gloves	a. Gesichts-/Atemmaske
2. goggles	b. Handschuhe
3. face mask	c. Schutzanzug
4. hard hat	d. Sicherheitsschuhe
5. protective overall	e. Schutzbrille
6. safety boots	f. Schutzhelm

2 Complete the description of picture 1 with the correct pieces of protective clothing.

Two workers, who are wearing red [1], are checking hazardous goods. In order not to breathe in dangerous gases they must wear [2]. To protect their hands and feet they are wearing [3] and [4]. The third worker is wearing a [5] to protect his or her head.

A | Safety precautions and warning signs

People who handle dangerous goods should not only wear protective clothing but also strictly follow safety precautions and warning signs. They therefore need to understand warning signs because false handling could lead to terrible accidents.

1 Speculate about the possible consequences if people are not careful in the following situations.

1. There is acid on the floor and you want to load goods.
2. Someone is smoking a cigarette near different gases.
3. You didn't see the warning sign that forklift trucks might cross your way.
4. The floor is covered with nails and you are not wearing safety boots.
5. A colleague is carrying goods, without gloves, that he should not touch.

P **2** A colleague says: "Wearing protective clothing when handling dangerous goods is totally unnecessary." List arguments against his view.

P **3** ⚠ Inform yourselves on the Internet about safety precautions when dealing with the goods below. Prepare a presentation and present your findings in class.

→ **PHRASES:** Presentations

acids • chemical liquids • detergents • eye-irritant substances • gases • pesticides • propane bottles • radioactive substances

4 **SAFETY FIRST** ⚠

Match the warning signs with the correct meanings. Then match the signs to the hazardous goods in exercise 3.

a. compressed gas	d. hazardous to the environment
b. corrosive substances	e. health risks
c. explosives	f. poisons

1

2

3

4

5

6

WORD BANK

acid – Säure
corrosive – ätzend
explosive – Sprengstoff
face mask – Gesichts-/Atemmaske
fume – Dampf
glove – Handschuh
goggles – Schutzbrille
hazardous goods – Gefahrengut
irritant – reizend, reizauslösend
lifting cart – Hubwagen
liquid – Flüssigkeit
poison – Gift
protective clothing – Schutzkleidung
safety boots – Sicherheitsschuhe
safety precaution – Sicherheits-vorkehrung
solid – Feststoff

B | Packing dangerous goods

When packing dangerous goods it is necessary to use the right packaging to keep products and workers safe. Sometimes the packaging has to resist aggressive chemicals or a fall from a great height.

1 Match the words with their German translations.

1. adhesive tape	a. auslaufen, entweichen
2. barrel	b. (in Flaschen) abfüllen
3. to bottle	c. etikettieren, kennzeichnen
4. cardboard box	d. Fass, Tonne
5. to label	e. Klebeband
6. to leak out	f. Pappkarton
7. safety can	g. Sicherheitsflasche, -kanister
8. UN number label	h. unbeschädigt
9. undamaged	i. UN Kennzahlaufkleber

R **2** KMK II ⊙ A 3.21

Während seiner Ausbildung arbeitet Hakan Bulut für drei Monate in einem Lagerhaus in den USA. Hakan muss über seinen Auslandsaufenthalt einen kurzen Erfahrungsbericht schreiben und macht sich dafür regelmäßig Notizen. Hören Sie ein Gespräch zwischen Hakan und Paul Gray, einem erfahrenen Packer. Füllen Sie auf Deutsch die folgende Tabelle mit Informationen aus, die Sie dem Hörtext entnehmen, damit Hakan diese dann für seinen Bericht verwenden kann.

Verpackungsart	Produktbeispiel	Begründung

R **3** KMK II ⊙ A 3.21

Hören Sie das Gespräch noch einmal und fassen Sie auf Deutsch Paul Grays Erklärung eines UN Kennzahlaufklebers zusammen. Erläutern Sie, wie dieser Aufkleber im Notfall helfen kann.

P **4**

Add at least one more product for each type of packaging in exercise 2. Explain why the products should be packed like this.

5 UNDERSTANDING TECHNICAL ENGLISH

Match the words with the signs. Then describe the differences between these types of signs and give at least one more example for each type of sign.

prohibition sign · warning sign · mandatory sign · emergency sign · fire safety sign

1

2

3

4

5

C | Loading hazardous goods

Dangerous goods not only have to be adequately packed, they also have to be loaded very carefully. Strict guidelines have to be followed in order to minimise health risks, product damage and dangers to the environment.

1 Look at the picture and speculate about the possible consequences for people and the environment in the case of illegal unloading of dangerous chemicals.

M **2** KMK II In Ihrer Firma haben sich in der Vergangenheit einige Unfälle beim Verladen von Gefahrengut ereignet. Ihre Vorgesetzte hat im Internet die folgenden Sicherheitshinweise gefunden und möchte diese gut sichtbar für alle Mitarbeiter an der Laderampe anbringen lassen. Sie bittet Sie zu diesem Zweck auf Grundlage des folgenden Textes einen Hinweiszettel auf Deutsch zu erstellen.

Sicherheitshinweise für das Verladen von Gefahrengut

1. …

ww#.guidelines.com

Guidelines for loading hazardous goods

- Remember that not all means of transport are suitable for the transportation of all types of products. Accordingly, the means of transport and carriers should be carefully chosen and checked first.
- Before loading a suitable vehicle with dangerous goods, check the following things:
  - All goods must be safely packed and correctly labelled.
  - Don't put too many goods on each pallet, so that they won't fall off during transport.
  - It is essential to use adequate cargo securing means (for example, lumber, metal bars or different types of lashing) to guarantee safe transport by ensuring that the goods cannot move.
- After you have loaded the goods, make sure that they are secured in the best possible way. An unsecured load may cause accidents and is difficult to unload. This may lead to damage to the packaging and the goods, and cause serious health risks. Moreover, product damage may be expensive for the business and unloading may take a long time.
- Finally, when you are loading hazardous goods you must follow safety precautions at the loading dock. The dock must be clean and not slippery. If trucks are used for transport they must be secured against rolling off during the process of loading. Furthermore, fall protection should be installed and it must be possible to use the stairs along the loading dock if necessary.

WORD BANK

bar – Stange, Bügel, Leiste
cargo – Fracht, Ladung
carrier – Frachtführer, Transportunternehmen
fall protection – Fallschutz
guideline – Richtlinie
lashing – Verschnürung
loading dock – Laderampe
means of transport – Transportmittel
pallet – Palette
safety can – Sicherheitsflasche, -kanister
securing means – sichernde Maßnahme(n)
UN number label – UN Kennzahlaufkleber
unloading – Entladen

F

NACH DIESEM MODUL:

- √ kann ich *Small Talk* auf Englisch machen,
- √ kenne ich die Regeln des *Small Talk,*
- √ kann ich auf Englisch Essen erklären und bestellen.

1

2

3

4

Socialising

Socialising is very important. It can strengthen relationships with your colleagues and improve the working atmosphere in a company. It can also be a good way of getting to know your customers or potential customers a little better. And in today's global world, English has become the world's language. So although the people you meet and work with are likely to come from a wide range of cultural backgrounds, you will often be required to communicate in English. That means that it is important to not only have the necessary language skills, but also the intercultural knowledge so that you can make a good first impression and develop professional and personal relationships.

I **1** **Look at the pictures above. What relationship do you think these people might have to each other? Discuss with your partner.**

2 **Brainstorm a list of topics these people might be talking about.**

P **3** **Choose one of the pictures and create a small dialogue.**

4 **Look at photo 1. Brainstorm what cultural misunderstandings could take place when a German employee meets a person from another country.**

P **5** **Make a list of situations when a German technician might have contact with foreign colleagues – for example, customers, suppliers, manufacturers, etc.**

A | Small talk

Your company has visitors from a subsidiary in Poland. Fabian, a German trainee, has been asked to show Jan, a Polish trainee, around the company.

1 A 1.5 **Listen to the dialogue between Jan and Fabian. Take notes of the topics the two are talking about. Then listen again and make a list of the phrases they use.**

2 **Name other topics that Jan and Fabian could also talk about.**

3 **Which of the following topics would / wouldn't you talk about? Why? Discuss in class.**

free-time activities • films you have recently seen • sex • your job or school course • politics • money • personal problems • fashion • sports • food • the boss's wife • the weather • your favourite music • religion

4 **Small talk is not that difficult. All that is needed is an 'ice breaker' to get things going. Look at the following examples and come up with appropriate answers.**

→ **PHRASES:** Socialising

In the workshop:
a. Did you see the game last night?
b. How was your weekend?
c. It's warm today, isn't it?

In the car:
a. How was your trip / flight?
b. Is this your first time in Germany?
c. How's the weather in Sao Paolo?

At a trade fair:
a. Did you have any problems finding our stand?
b. Would you like a brochure?
c. If you like, I could give you a demonstration.

In the canteen:
a. Have you tried the tiramisu? It's amazing!
b. Is anybody sitting here?
c. Ah! I see you like spicy food.

5 **Now it's your turn to break the ice! Think of at least three ice breakers for each of the following situations:**

→ **PHRASES:** Socialising

1. You are at a bar with colleagues on Friday evening.
2. You work with a new colleague one afternoon.
3. You are at the "Green Technology" conference. It's time for a coffee break.
4. You've just arrived at work and you're in the lift. A person you don't know enters.

6 **Choose one of the four situations above. Start a conversation and try to keep it going for as long as possible. Then end the conversation politely and act it out in front of the class.**

→ **PHRASES:** Socialising

7 **Check the Internet and create your own 'Dos & Don'ts' guide to making small talk and present it to your class. Also include some intercultural aspects.**

Dos	Don'ts
Make eye contact.	Ask personal questions.

WORD BANK

subsidiary – Tochtergesellschaft
trainee – Auszubildende(r)

B | Small talk in business

R **1** KMK II

Ihr Arbeitgeber hat im Internet folgenden Artikel gefunden. Da er nur wenig Englisch kann, bittet er Sie, die folgenden Fragen auf Deutsch zu beantworten.

1. Was wird oft in abwertender Weise über Small Talk gesagt?
2. Was passiert, wenn man sich nicht am Small Talk beteiligt?
3. Was sind die positiven Auswirkungen von Small Talk?

Small talk in business

Small talk is often dismissed as a waste of time, or as the art of saying nothing with a lot of words. Some people say it has no place in the business world, since the subjects discussed are often 'unimportant' – i.e. the weather, sports, fashion or other trivial matters. However, if you don't take part in small talk, your business partners might feel that you are being unfriendly or antisocial. When people just stand next to one another, without any signs of communication between them, it can lead to a feeling of uneasiness, and even tension. And this is certainly not good for future business or private relations. Small talk is in fact a very important and effective tool for avoiding an awkward silence between people who don't know each other, especially business partners who may want to form a relationship. Making small talk with strangers helps to break the ice; you discover what they like or dislike, so you can find a common ground of some sort. It helps, for example, if you support the same football team, like the same kind of car, or read the same kinds of books. However, it is also important to know who you are making small talk with. The rules of small talk are not international and different cultures have their own dos and don'ts. For example, you may have been told to always make eye contact when talking to your counterpart – but this may offend a material supplier in China. If you are going to have contact with someone from a different cultural background it is a good idea to do a little research to avoid any embarassing mistakes.

M **2** KMK II

Ihr Arbeitgeber bittet Sie, für die Mitarbeiter stichwortartig ein kurzes Merkblatt anhand dieses Textes auf Deutsch zu erstellen.

R **3**

Sind Sie ein guter Smalltalker? Bewerten Sie die Aussagen zum Small Talk in einem Online-Test mit „Yes" oder „No". Notieren Sie die entsprechenden Buchstaben.

Statements	Yes	No
1. Small talk deals with rather unimportant topics. Another word for it is chitchat.	a	c
2. Religion always makes a good topic, because it is controversial.	d	e
3. Answering questions with 'yes' or 'no' during small talk is appropriate.	i	e
4. A good answer when asked if you'd like something to drink is: "I'd love a cup of coffee, thank you."	g	h
5. "That's great" is an acceptable answer to the statement: "I got the job!"	b	i
6. The noun "talk" can also mean speech.	a	c
7. Small talk is an icebreaker.	b	f

Addieren Sie die Buchstabenwerte a = 3, b = 3, c = 1, d = 0, e = 3, f = 1, g = 3, h = 1, i = 1.
Wer hat die höchste Zahl? (Maximum 21)

C | Eating out

1 Look at the German words (1.–16.) below and match them with the English equivalent (a.–p.).

1. Speisekarte	a. well-done
2. Rechnung	b. pork
3. Rind	c. side order
4. Vorspeise	d. bill
5. Schweinefleisch	e. game
6. Wild	f. dessert
7. durchgebraten	g. savoury
8. Hauptgericht	h. fork
9. Geflügel	i. menu
10. Kellner(in)	j. main dish
11. Nachtisch	k. beef
12. Trinkgeld	l. poultry
13. Beilage	m. starter
14. vegetarisch	n. waiter / waitress
15. herzhaft	o. vegetarian
16. Gabel	p. tip

M **2** Partner 1: You are taking a foreign colleague out to dinner in a traditional German restaurant. Study the menu below and explain the dishes to him / her.
Partner 2: Take the role of the foreign colleague and ask questions about the menu.

Gasthaus Sonne

Tagesmenu (10,95 €)

Vorspeisen
Lauchcremesuppe ***oder*** *kleiner gemischter Salat*

***

Hauptgerichte
Rinderrouladen mit Kartoffelklößen & Sauerkraut
oder
Putenschnitzel mit Pommes Frites
oder
Forelle Müllerin mit Salzkartoffeln

***

Nachtisch
Rote Grütze mit Sahne ***oder*** *Gemischtes Eis*
(Vanille / Erdbeere / Schoko)

Inklusive ein alkoholfreies Getränk (0,3 l)

WORD BANK

avoid (v) – vermeiden
awkward – unangenehm
common ground – gemeinsame Basis
dismiss (v) sth. as – etwas abtun als
tension – Spannung
trivial – unbedeutend
uneasiness – Unbehagen

3 Now the two of you are ready to order. The young German waitress / waiter doesn't mind taking the order in English. Study the eating out phrases at the end of the book and create a role play. Practise, and perform it in front of the class.

→ **PHRASES:** Socialising

07

NACH DIESEM MODUL:

- ✓ kann ich auf Englisch verschiedene Transportmittel sowie deren Vor- und Nachteile beschreiben,
- ✓ kann ich auf Englisch die Organisation von Warentransporten erläutern,
- ✓ kann ich auf Englisch Dokumente und Incoterms benennen und erklären.

1

2

3

4

Shipping goods

Shipping goods requires careful planning. In particular, questions about the kind of goods, the schedule and the final destination need to be answered when preparing for the shipping of goods.

1 **Look at the pictures and complete the following text about the route of the goods to their destination. Use the words from the box.**

deliver • destination port • loading dock • ship • stored • truck

Your company wants to **1** goods to a customer in Halifax, Canada. First the goods have to be transported to Rotterdam by **2**. At the **3** they are loaded onto a **4** which takes them to the **5**, where the goods are **6** for the customer to collect.

2 **Make a list of the means of transport that you know.**

P **3** **Talk to your partner about what products your company ships and to which destinations. Say which means of transport are used for them.**

WATCH OUT!
The term 'shipping' not only means transportation by ship – it refers to all means of transport.

A | Different means of transport

Choosing the right means of transport is important because transportation is a major cost factor. However, you shouldn't just use the cheapest means of transport, especially when your goods are perishable or need to arrive quickly.

1 Collect possible advantages and disadvantages of different means of transport. Then read the text and check your ideas.

Means of transport

Goods must be transported efficiently and according to the customer's wishes. There are four types of carriers: railroads, waterways, roads and planes.

Railroads are used more and more for carrying freight. Trains can transport both heavy and light products and are environmentally friendly. There are refrigerator wagons for perishables. Hazardous or urgent goods can be shipped by rail, too.

Waterway carriers offer cheap and environmentally friendly transportation, in particular of bulky, heavy and hazardous goods. Disadvantages are that seaworthy packing is needed to protect the goods and that it is rather slow.

Road carriers are not used for bulky, low-value goods. But they can offer door-to-door delivery and they reach places other carriers cannot get to. Special lorries can transport liquids, refrigerator trucks are used for perishables and vans are often used for furniture.

Air freight is used for goods which have to arrive quickly. Examples are urgent medicines, spare parts and perishables. The main disadvantage is the high cost.

2 Match the means of transport with the most suitable goods. Give reasons.

1. air transport	a. clothing from Austria to Switzerland
2. rail transport	b. furniture from Hamburg to Braunschweig
3. road transport	c. 30 trucks from Madrid, Spain to New York, USA
4. sea transport	d. urgent medicine from Munich to Sydney, Australia

3 Compare the different means of transport using the words in the box.

cheap • environmentally friendly • expensive • fast • reliable • risky • slow

WORD BANK

air freight – Luftfracht
bulky goods – Sperrgut
carrier – Beförderungsunternehmen, Frachtführer
consignment – Warensendung
deliver (v) – zustellen, liefern
destination – Bestimmungsort
fragile – zerbrechlich
freight – Fracht
hazardous – gefährlich
label (v) – etikettieren, kennzeichnen, beschriften
load (v) – (ver)laden
loading dock – Ladedock
means of transport – Transportmittel
overseas – Übersee
packing – Versandverpackung
perishable – (leicht) verderblich
refrigerator wagon – Kühlwaggon
seaworthy – seefest
ship (v) – versenden, verschiffen
shipment – Versand, Verschiffung
urgent – dringend, eilig
waterway – Wasserweg

B | Organising transportation

Before goods are transported, you have to reach an agreement with the customer on the schedule, the costs, the means of transport and the packing material.

1 Match the words with the correct definitions.

1. consignment	a. easily broken
2. fragile	b. freight that is sent somewhere
3. to label	c. other countries across the sea
4. overseas	d. place where goods are stored
5. warehouse	e. when you put information on something

R **2** Listen to the dialogue between the storemen Tom and Luke. Answer the questions.
A 3.22

1. Which goods do they have to prepare for transportation?
2. Which country is the consignment going to be shipped to?
3. How must the goods be packed?
4. Why is it important to talk to the customer before the goods are shipped?

P **3** When you organise transport you should also think about possible environmental costs. First explain what 'environmental costs' might be. Then collect ideas about the causes of environmental costs. Report to the class.

P **4** Search the Internet for information about the causes and costs of the following disasters. Prepare a short presentation and present your results to the class.

→ **PHRASES:** Presentations

Hurricane Katrina hitting New Orleans in 2005 • floods and droughts in China in 2010/2011 • Exxon Valdez oil spill in 1989

P **5** Discuss this statement: "It's fair that road carriers have to pay some of the environmental costs they are causing."

6 UNDERSTANDING TECHNICAL ENGLISH
The words 'carrier', 'dock(s)' and 'to load' have various meanings. Use a dictionary and translate the following sentences.

1. We are an international carrier that transports goods to Spain.
2. The production company knows a carrier that provides various services.
3. Sue is waiting for a delivery at the dock.
4. We arrived at the docks on time.
5. It took an hour to load the truck.
6. I need to load paper into the printer.

C | Documentation in foreign trade

In foreign trade, different documents clarify aspects such as description, quality, number, means of transport, indemnity and inspection. Incoterms (terms of delivery) are used for contracts in international trade. They make clear who bears what risks and costs for the goods at each point during transport.

1 Match the documents with the correct definitions.

1. air waybill
2. bill of lading
3. certificate of origin
4. commercial invoice
5. insurance certificate
6. packing list

a. document giving details of the goods sent
b. invoice issued by the seller to the buyer
c. document issued by the insurance company insuring the freight against risks
d. document issued by the shipping company for the goods shipped and signed by the carrier
e. documents that the goods have been received for shipment by air
f. shows the country of origin of the goods or the country where they were mainly produced

/P **2** Read the information on pages 85–86. Choose three Incoterms and take turns asking your partner what they mean and who bears what risks and costs.

3 Which documents for foreign trade are used in your company? Report to the class.

4 Look at page IV and convert the following imperial measurements into metric measurements. Compare your answers with your partner and read them out.

1. 14 feet
2. 2,100 pounds
3. 10 inches
4. 40 miles
5. 30,500 lbs
6. 340 oz

5 MK III Ihr Betrieb überlegt in Rotterdam ein Warenlager zu eröffnen, um die günstige verkehrstechnische Lage für die Verschiffung von Gütern zu nutzen. Verfassen Sie eine formgerechte Anfrage per E-Mail an Ihren in Rotterdam ansässigen Spediteur (Herr Steinbach, E-Mail: k.steinbach@logistics...com) mit folgendem Inhalt:

- Wählen Sie eine passende Betreffzeile und Anrede.
- Informieren Sie Herrn Steinbach über die Pläne Ihrer Firma.
- Erkundigen Sie sich nach der Größe des Containerhafens. Fragen Sie nach der Anzahl der Terminals und ob Binnen- und Tiefseeschiffahrt dort abgefertigt werden.
- Da Ihnen eine schnelle Abfertigung wichtig ist, möchten Sie wissen, wie das Be- und Entladen von Containern erfolgt.
- Beenden Sie Ihre Anfrage formgerecht.

WORD BANK

airway bill – Luftfrachtbrief
bear (v) – tragen
bill of lading – Konnossement
certificate of origin – Ursprungszeugnis
commercial invoice – Handelsrechnung
contract – Vertrag
environmental costs – Umweltkosten
foreign trade – Außenhandel
indemnity – Schadensersatz
inspection – Prüfung, Kontrolle
insurance certificate – Versicherungspolice
invoice – Rechnung
issue (v) – ausstellen, anfertigen
measure – Maß
packing list – Packliste
packing material – Verpackungsmaterial
storeman – Lagerist, Lagerverwalter
terms of delivery – Lieferbedingungen

→ **PHRASES:** Written communication

G

NACH DIESEM MODUL:

- ✓ kann ich eine englische Präsentation vorbereiten,
- ✓ kann ich auf Englisch präsentieren.

1

2

3

4

Presentations

At some point in your career you may be required to present your company, or their products or services, either informally or on a more formal level. This could mean presenting a new product to a potential customer, or presenting the company as a whole, or something more specific, such as assembly instructions or a positional sketch. Whatever you may be presenting, the ability to give an oral presentation is a key skill. It is also a skill that can be developed and improved.

P **1** Look at the pictures above and describe them using the words below.

to present · meeting · flipchart · graph · chart · laptop · preparation · to explain · sales pitch · audience · projector

P **2** For what reasons might you have to give a presentation? Write a list.

3 With a partner, decide upon a final list and share it with the class.

4 With the same partner brainstorm what you think is important to remember when giving a presentation. Write your answers in a word web like the one below.

A | Preparing a presentation

1 **In the following table are words which are linked to presentations. Match the English words (1.–10.) with the appropriate German words (a.–j.).**

1. audience	a. Augenkontakt
2. prompt cards	b. beschreiben
3. body language	c. Zusammenfassung
4. eye contact	d. visuelle Hilfsmittel
5. handout	e. Publikum
6. to prepare	f. Schaubild
7. graph	g. Stichwortkarten
8. visual aids	h. Körpersprache
9. to describe	i. vorbereiten
10. summary	j. Informationsblatt

M **2** KMK II **Fassen Sie den folgenden Text über die Vorbereitung einer Präsentation unter Beantwortung folgender Fragen auf Deutsch zusammen.**

1. Warum soll eine Präsentation nicht schriftlich ausformuliert werden?
2. Wie soll eine Präsentation gegliedert sein?
3. Was ist „signposting“?
4. Welche Vorteile bieten visuelle Hilfsmittel?
5. Wie müssen Präsentationsfolien aussehen, damit sie wirken?

How to make a presentation

You have been asked by your boss to give a presentation? Here are a few tips:

→ Do not write out your presentation in full. Instead, use numbered prompt cards with key words – they are the best way to remember important points.
→ Remember: your presentation needs to have an introduction, a main part, and a conclusion.
→ Begin by giving a brief overview of the points to be covered.
→ Use "signposting" phrases to lead through your presentation, e.g.:

> I would like to begin by ... • Let me start by showing you ... • Next, I would like to say something about ... • Another important point is ... • Finally, I will talk about ... • In conclusion, ...

→ Always finish with a conclusion.

Visual aids

You can use visual aids, such as Powerpoint, to help reinforce what you say. Visual aids help you explain complicated ideas or technical details more easily and hold the interest of your audience. They also make your presentation look more professional.
If necessary, you can print them out and use them as a handout for the audience. Visual aids could include graphs, pictures, plans, diagrams, or short texts. However, if you do use your visual aids to show text, then follow these guidelines:

→ Limit the text to six lines.
→ Try to use no more than six words per line.
→ Print the text in large letters, using upper and lower case letters.
→ Use dark colours, such as black, red, blue, or green. Light colours are difficult to read.

WORD BANK

assembly – Montage
positional sketch – Technologieschema

3 Match the visual aids (1. – 6) with the pictures below (a. – e.).

1. plan 2. pie chart 3. line graph 4. bar chart 5. diagram 6. table

a.

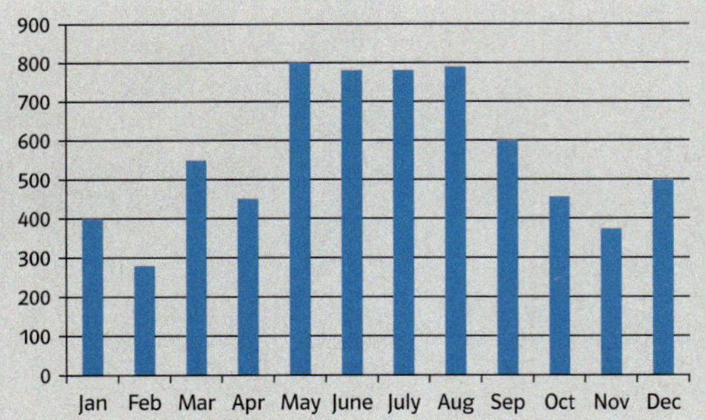

b.

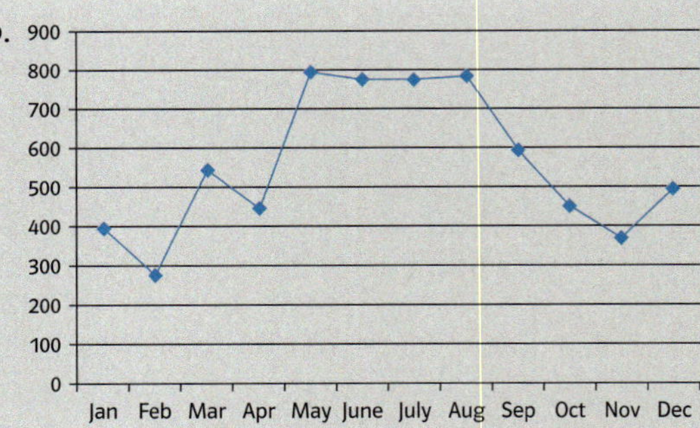

c.

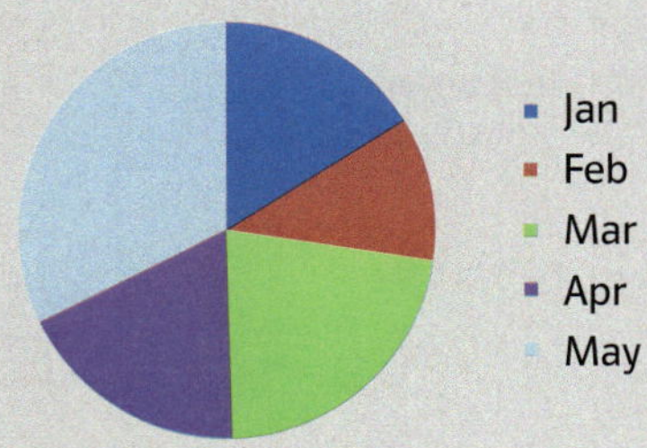

d.

2012		
Jan	$1,256	–6%
Feb	$1,477	+4%
Mar	$1,288	–5%
Apr	$1,543	+9%

e.

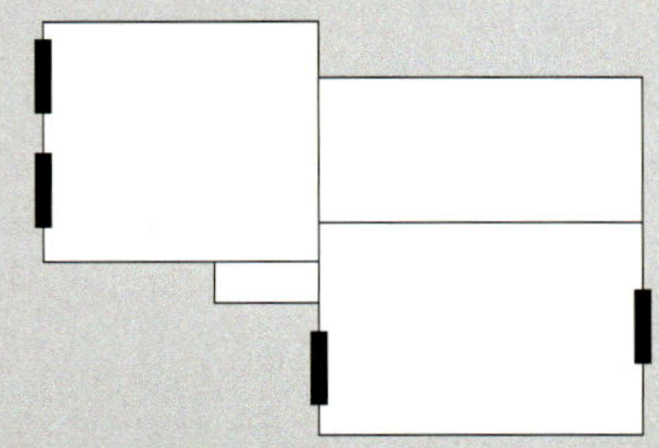

f.

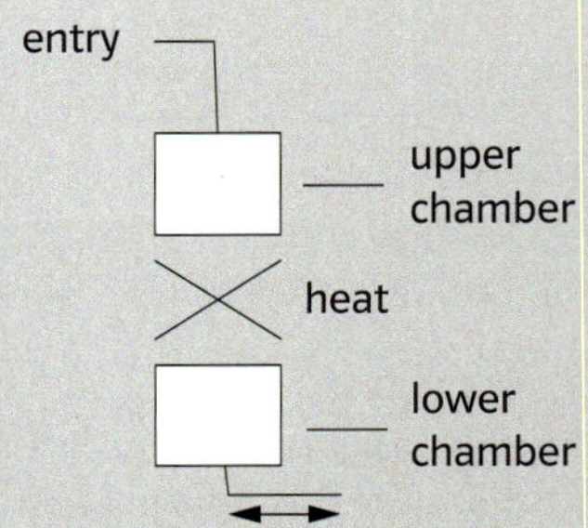

B | Describing materials and products

P **1** Think of something that you often use and describe it by using the terms in the box to help you. Don't name the item you are describing. Try and write 3 to 5 sentences.

I **2** Take it in turns to read your sentences to each other and see if you can guess what your partner is describing.

INFO BOX: Useful phrases for describing materials and products

It is a	strong · sturdy · rigid · flexible · lightweight · shiny · robust · matt	material.
The design is	modern · state-of-the-art · classic · elegant · old-fashioned.	
It is	user-friendly · difficult to operate · reliable · innovative · hand-crafted.	

C | Delivering a presentation

R **1**
◎ A 1.6

Max Wiesinger, a trained carpenter who works for a furniture design company, is presenting a new line of furniture at a trade show. Listen to the presentation and complete the following text.

Good morning ladies and gentleman. Today **1** our new range of **2**, *Simply Wood*. The range, which is shown here on the first slide, includes chairs, a large table, a lounger, and benches. I would like to start by talking about the **3** used in the furniture. All of the *Simply Wood* range is made from single softwood timber and has been **4** by our highly-skilled carpenters and joiners. If you look at this picture, you can see that the benches and the seats are designed with a low back, deep seats and long arms to offer a great deal of comfort and convenience. Thanks to a special varnish, the furniture is 100 % **5** and will not suffer from discolouring. **6** from this final slide, the furniture is also available in white, to give it a classic, timeless look. And do not worry, we have used a durable white polyurethane coating that is suitable for every environment. On your handout you will see more details about each piece, including the measurements. **7** this morning. Are there any questions? Yes …

P **2**

Now it's your turn. Work in small groups and design a chair, a pocket torch, or any other object of your choice. Present your ideas in class. Use the following words and phrases to help you:

→ **PHRASES:** Presentations

We have designed a … • Our idea was to … • Our design is made of … • The advantage of the material we used is … • Its measurements are … • length • diameter • weight • width • height • rectangular • circle • circular • square • smooth edges • glued/screwed together • made out of one piece

M **3**
KMK I

Ihre Kollegin muss nächste Woche eine wichtige Präsentation halten und bittet Sie um Ihre Hilfe. Sie hat den folgenden Text gefunden, versteht aber leider nur wenig Englisch. Übertragen Sie den Text für sie sinngemäß ins Deutsche.

7 Ways to Do it Right: Presentations

1. Keep it short and simple (KISS).
2. Do not use too many visual aids.
3. If you are presenting in a group, decide beforehand who will say what.
4. Practice at least once in front of an audience.
5. Do not read from your notes. Look at your audience.
6. Structure your presentation with phrases so your audience can follow more easily.
7. Tell the audience when they can ask questions – either during the presentation, or at the end.

WORD BANK

carpenter – Tischler(in) / Schreiner(in)
circle – Kreis
circular – kreisförmig
diameter – Dicke
furniture – Möbel
height – Höhe
length – Länge
rectangular – rechteckig
smooth – glatt
square – quadratisch
trade show – Messe
weight – Gewicht
width – Breite

WORD BANK ◎

durable – haltbar
joiner – Tischler(in) / Schreiner(in)
polyurethane coating – Polyurethan-beschichtung
softwood – Weichholz
timber – Holz
varnish – Lack

08

NACH DIESEM MODUL:

- ✓ kann ich auf Englisch Ziele beim Umgang mit Abfällen nennen,
- ✓ kann ich auf Englisch Möglichkeiten der Müllvermeidung und -beseitigung aufzeigen,
- ✓ kann ich auf Englisch Umweltverschmutzung durch Schiffe erklären.

1

2

3

4

Waste disposal and the environment

Environmental awareness and waste management have become important issues both in industry and in our private lives. Many people agree that we must protect our environment and improve the quality of life. Additionally, there is waste legislation which regulates how waste should be handled within the European Community.

1 **Look at the pictures and match them with the correct captions.**

a. Industrial waste disposal
b. Metal and aluminium cans before transportation to a recycling plant
c. Labelling symbol showing that a product is environmentally friendly
d. Recycling bins for paper, metal, plastic and glass waste

2 **Read the text about the 'green dot' and choose the correct words.**

The 'green dot' is a **1** (logo / written text) which you can find on many **2** (products / packaging materials). It tells you that they **3** (shouldn't be put in recycling bins / can be recycled). Most people collect **4** (household waste / industrial waste) labelled with the 'green dot' in **5** (blue / yellow) bags.

P **3** **Talk about what you do to protect the environment.**

A | Waste management

In the past most waste was just taken to a landfill. But in recent years it has been recognised that we should try to reduce the production of waste and that some waste contains materials which can be recycled.

1 Match the words to their German equivalents.

1. to avoid	a. entsorgen
2. to deal with	b. Entsorgungsunternehmen
3. to dispose of	c. Transportmittel
4. environmental impact	d. umgehen mit
5. means of transport	e. Umweltauswirkung
6. waste disposal firm	f. vermeiden

R **2** Ms Hughes, head storewoman of a warehouse, is answering questions about waste management during a visit at a vocational school. Listen and complete the sentences.

⦾ A 3.23

1. Mrs Hughes says that it is a very important first step to …
2. The environmental impact can be reduced by …
3. Waste should be recycled and put back …
4. Mrs Hughes asks the students what they do with …
5. One of the students explains that he collects them and then …
6. Sometimes it is better not to recycle waste because …

3 Read the text and decide if the statements on page 66 are true or false. Correct the false statements.

ww#.wastedisposal.com

The disposal of one-way packaging

The German government passed a packaging law in 1991 that forces producers to deal with the recycling or disposal of the packaging they sell. Household packaging is only collected if the producers have paid a licence fee and put on the green dot logo. Consumers put this packaging into a sack or bin which is collected by special waste collection vehicles and later recycled. When one-way packaging is used in industry, the producers usually ask waste disposal firms to collect and either recycle or dispose of it.

Multi-way packaging

Some packaging can be used more than once. For example, drinks suppliers take part in a returnable system in which consumers can return deposit bottles. The bottles are then transported back to the producer who cleans and refills them. An example in industry are suppliers cooperating with pallet pool operators, who rent pallets to them and take them back later.

Disposal of industrial waste

Some industrial processes produce byproducts that can be recycled or used by other companies. But in some cases industrial waste cannot be recycled or it is more environmentally friendly to dispose of it.

WORD BANK

bin – Behälter
directive – Richtlinie
environmental awareness – Umweltbewusstsein
hazardous – gefährlich
industrial waste – Industrieabfälle
label (v) – etikettieren, kennzeichnen, beschriften
multi-way packaging – Mehrwegverpackung
one-way packaging – Einwegverpackung
packaging law – Verpackungsverordnung
pallet pool operator – Palettenverleihbetreiber
recycling plant – Recyclinganlage
returnable system – Rücknahmesystem
supplier – Lieferant, Zulieferer
waste disposal firm – Müll-/Abfallentsorgungsunternehmen
waste legislation – Abfallgesetzgebung

1. In 1991 a law was passed by the EU that asks producers to deal with the recycling or disposal of the packaging they sell.
2. Producers have to pay a fee to put the green dot logo on their package labelling.
3. Consumers have to bring empty one-way packages back to the places where they bought the products.
4. A returnable system means that the supplier returns the packaging to the producer and the producer can use it again.
5. Multi-way packaging means that the packaging can be used a number of times.
6. In industry some suppliers cooperate with pallet pool operators who sell pallets and take them back later.
7. If byproducts are produced in industrial processes they always have to be disposed of.

P/I **4** **Inform yourself about how waste is handled at your company or school. Discuss your findings with a partner and present them in class.**

5 **Complete the text about the pallet pool system with the words from the box.**

collects • cycle • depot • environmentally friendly • examined • returnable • operator • pallet pool

The 1 system is a 2 system where the 3 delivers pallets to the company that rents them. The company ships the pallets with the goods to the customers and informs the pool operator where the pallets have been shipped to. Then the operator 4 the empty pallets. When the pallets are back at the 5, they are 6 and repaired, if necessary, before the 7 starts again. The system itself is also 8 as the total number of pallets is reduced.

P **6** **What are possible advantages or disadvantages of the pallet pool system? Work with a partner and make a list.**

7 **Look at the verbs in brackets and use the gerund where necessary.**

Example:
(Dispose) of waste is a global issue. → Disposing of waste is a global issue.

1. I always try to think of ways of (avoid) waste at home.
2. We should not (pollute) our environment any more.
3. Frank believes in (use) environmentally friendly products.
4. People must (put) old newspapers into special recycling bins.
5. (Use) less packaging is an important aim of many producers.
6. Remember (buy) products that can be recycled.

B | EU waste legislation

1 Complete the text about the EU directive of waste with the correct words.

The EU has **1** (legislation/logistics) to protect the environment and human health by avoiding the **2** (positive/hazardous) effects of waste production and management. Producers or holders of waste must deal with it themselves or ask waste disposal **3** (suppliers/firms) to do so. EU member states may **4** (cooperate/protect) to create a network of waste **5** (packaging/disposal) facilities. Dangerous waste **6** (must not/should) be mixed and must be packed and labelled in line with EU **7** (regulations/awareness).

P **2** The EU wants its member states to improve the handling of waste in line with a given order of priority. Search the Internet for the 'directive of waste' and take notes on the priorities. Discuss them and decide whether or not you agree with them.

C | Environmental awareness

R **1** KMK III In Ihrem Betrieb wird überlegt, aus ökologischen Gründen weniger Güter per Schiff zu transportieren. Ihr Chef hat den folgenden Artikel über die Umweltverschmutzung durch Schiffe gefunden. Beantworten Sie seine Fragen zum Text auf Deutsch.

1. Was genau sind *black water* und *grey water*?
2. Welche Rolle spielt der von Schiffen verursachte Lärm?
3. Welche weiteren Gefahren gehen von Schiffen für die Meerestiere aus?
4. Was sagt der Text über die Wirkung strenger Umweltgesetze?

The environmental impact of shipping goods

Up to 40% of air pollution is produced by CO_2 emissions of ships' diesel engines. Ships also cause pollution by oil leaking into the water, where it can kill fish and other animals. In addition, so-called 'black water' is dumped into the sea every day. 'Black water' is sewage from toilets, which can contain bacteria and damage people's health. 'Grey water' pollutes the sea, too. This is waste water from cleaning activities on ships. Finally, there is solid waste, such as glass, paper, aluminium and plastics, which is dangerous for fish or birds. Another form of pollution often played down is noise pollution. The noise that ships produce can travel long distances across the sea and cause problems for animals that use sound for their orientation, communication and feeding. Ship collisions with large sea creatures can occur and marine life might be injured or even die. Despite strict environmental laws, there are still many ship owners who are charged with environmental violations every year.

2 UNDERSTANDING TECHNICAL ENGLISH

Look at the text again and form word pairs with the words from the box.

air • CO_2 • diesel • noise • solid • violations • waste

WORD BANK

dump (v) – verklappen, verladen
pollution – Verschmutzung
regulation – Vorschrift
take measures – Maßnahmen ergreifen

H

NACH DIESEM MODUL:

- ✓ kann ich auf Englisch auf Kundenbeschwerden reagieren,
- ✓ kann ich auf Englisch mit unzufriedenen Kunden umgehen.

Dealing with customers

The way a company deals with its customers is the key to its success. Whether you are arranging appointments, handling enquiries, or dealing with complaints, it is essential that you are able to express yourself clearly, confidently, and politely. And remember: the customer may not always be right, but they are very important.

1 Brainstorm words that describe what is shown in the photos above.

P **2** Compare your list of words with your partner and work together to describe the pictures. Use these words to help you:

complaint • hotline • builder • hard hat • building site • meeting • customer • plans • mechanic • explain • repairs • bonnet • overalls • engine

3 Which of the customers above do you think are happy, and which are unhappy? Explain your answer.

P **4** In what situations do you deal with customers in your job? Copy and complete the word web below to brainstorm reasons for talking to customers.

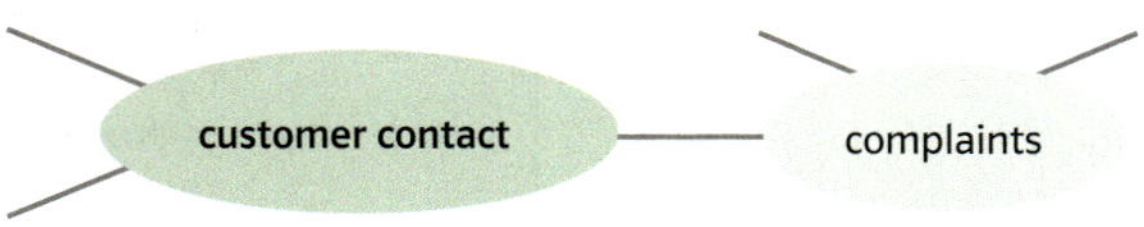

A | Complaints

1 Match the common causes for complaint on the left with the suggested solutions on the right. Several options may be appropriate.

1. delay in delivery	a. offer a price reduction
2. faulty goods	b. improve the service
3. damaged goods	c. repair the goods
4. unsatisfactory services	d. replace the goods
5. wrong goods	e. send the goods by air freight
6. too many/too few goods received	f. send the missing goods
7. too early delivery	g. take the goods back
	h. collect the surplus goods
	i. send a credit note

P **2** What about your industry? Which are the most common reasons for complaints? Make a list and compare it with a partner. Be as specific as possible.

R **3** Which of the following phrases are used for making complaints and which ones for replying to complaints? Make a list.

→ **PHRASES:** Dealing with customers

1. This is very inconvenient for us because we need the goods urgently.
2. We are sorry for any inconvenience this has caused.
3. We will keep the damaged goods until we hear from you.
4. Please return the damaged goods at our expense.
5. We can assure you that this will not happen again.
6. Some items were badly damaged.
7. We regret to inform you that the order has not yet arrived.
8. We think the damage may have occurred in transit.
9. We are experiencing difficulties with our new logistics software.
10. Could you please look into this problem immediately?
11. Please accept our apologies.
12. The reason for the mistake is that we are extremely busy at this time of the year.
13. Please send us replacements as soon as possible.
14. We hope that this proposal will find your approval.
15. We believe the problem is down to human error.

R **4** KMK II ⦾ A 1.7

You work for *Deutsches Netz*, an IT company in Hamburg. Your boss, Mr Bauder, receives a voicemail message on his mobile phone from Mr Jenkins, owner of *New Wave Marketing*, a subsidiary of an English marketing company based in Hamburg. Listen to the message and answer the following questions.

1. What did the technicians from Deutsches Netz do for New Wave Marketing?
2. What problems are the employees having (three things)?
3. What is the most serious problem?
4. Why is this a serious problem?
5. How should Mr Bauder contact Mr Jenkins?

WORD BANK

bonnet – Motorhaube
builder – Bauarbeiter
building site – Baustelle
hotline – Informationsdienst
repairs – Reparaturen
technician – Techniker(in)

P **5** **Mr Bauder asks you to respond to Mr Jenkins' phone call. He sends you the following email and asks you to draft a short email to the customer.**

→ **PHRASES:**
Dealing with customers

Von: mailto:s.bauder@DNetz...de
An: mailto:info@DNetz...de
Betreff: Bitte an Herrn Jenkins schreiben (eilt!!)

... diese Firma ist ein sehr wichtiger Kunde von uns und wir wollen ihn **auf keinen Fall** verlieren!! Bitte sagen Sie ihm folgendes:

- Es tut uns sehr leid, dass es diese Probleme gegeben hat.
- Wir verstehen völlig, dass es jetzt sehr ungelegen und ärgerlich ist.
- Wir vermuten, dass das Problem durch menschliches Versagen verursacht wurde.
- Wir werden sofort jemanden schicken, um das Netzwerk zu reparieren. (selbstverständlich auf unsere Kosten!)
- Der Techniker wird spätestens um 17 Uhr dort sein.

Bringen Sie nochmals unser Bedauern für das Problem zum Ausdruck und versichern Sie ihm, dass sich dies nicht wiederholen wird.

Danke,
Bauder

M **6** **You work for a plumbing and heating installation company in Leipzig. Your supervisor, Mr Hüber, receives an email about a recent job done for an American family living in the area. Your supervisor does not speak very good English and asks you to read the email and to sum it up in German.**

Von: mailto:j.t.levine@kwq...net
An: mailto:info@sippelheizung_sanitaer...net
Betreff: Problems with the heating

Dear Mr Hüber,

I am writing in reference to the heating system installed by your company at my house last week. Unfortunately, my family and I have been having some problems. Firstly, the water in the bathroom takes a long time to warm up – sometimes over 5 minutes!

Secondly, the temperature in the house is too low, and I cannot make it warmer. Also, I cannot find the instruction manual – did your technician take it with him? My final problem is that the underfloor heating does not seem to be working in the bathroom. The tiles on the floor are still cold in the morning. Is something wrong?

As it is winter, and very cold, I would ask you to send someone to my house as soon as possible to find a solution to these problems. Please give me a call, or send me an email to confirm.

Thank you in advance,

John Levine

B | Customer service

P **1** What five tips would you give a colleague about dealing with unhappy customers?

2 Compare your list with a partner.

How to deal with unhappy customers

**No company has happy customers 100 % of the time.
Things can always go wrong and customers can become unhappy – or worse, upset. Here are some tips on how to avoid making the situation worse.**

Stay calm: The customer may be angry at somebody, but it does not help the situation if you get just as angry. The last thing you want to do is start an argument – that is very unprofessional and unhelpful. Try to calm the customer down.

Listen, listen, listen: You will only be able to understand what has upset the customer if you listen, and listen carefully. Before you start talking, listen actively to the customer until you fully understand why they are unhappy. If you don't know what's wrong, you will not be able to do anything about it.

The customer is king: Show the customer that they, and their problem, are important to you. Tell them quickly how sorry you are for their problem and reassure them that you will do everything you can to help them. And, always be patient and polite.

Stay positive: Do your best to stay positive at all times. Remember that your goal is to solve the problem and you can do this better if you have a positive frame of mind. Regardless of how negative and furious the customer gets, it is important that you do not let it affect your mood.

No excuses: No matter what the problem is, or who you think caused it, do not blame other people or try to make excuses. Instead, take the initiative and do whatever you can to solve the problem.

R **3** Find the synonyms in the text for the following words and expressions:

1. to stop sth. from happening
2. disagreement
3. to aim
4. to fix
5. attitude
6. very angry
7. reason
8. to take control

R **4** KMK II Sie lesen den oben stehenden Artikel im Internet. Beantworten Sie die folgenden Fragen dazu in ganzen Sätzen auf Deutsch.

1. Warum ist es wichtig zu wissen, wie man mit unzufriedenen Kunden umgeht?
2. Was sollte man tun, wenn der Kunde sehr verärgert ist?
3. Warum ist es wichtig, dem Kunden ganz genau zuzuhören?
4. Wie kann man einem Kunden zeigen, dass man sein Problem ernst nimmt?
5. Wann ist es gerechtfertigt, jemand anderem die Schuld für das vorliegende Problem zu geben?

I **5** Choose one of the problems you listed in exercise A1 and create a short role play. One of you should play the unhappy / angry customer and the other the employee. Act out your role play in front of the class.

WORD BANK

instruction manual – Bedienungsanleitung
plumbing and heating – Heizung und Sanitär
underfloor heating – Fußbodenheizung

V1 Company tour

lingua tv

Before watching

1. Describe the photo.
2. Who do you think the men in the picture are?

While watching

3. Watch the film and find out the following:
   a. the number of countries SAND Machinery delivers to.
   b. the names of three departments that the men have visited.
   c. the number of people who work for the company.
   d. whether SAND Machinery has other sites and if so, where they are.
4. Watch the film again and answer the questions.
   a. What will Mr Kramer's main tasks be during the internship?
   b. What is made at the company's production site?

After watching

5. Explain the sentences from the clip in your own words.
   a. "I'm eager to get in and get my feet wet."
   b. "... around the globe, around the clock."

V2 Telephoning

lingua tv

Before watching

1. Describe the photo.

While watching

2. What problem does Ralf have at the beginning of the call?
3. Watch the film again and answer the questions.
   a. Who is calling?
   b. Who does he want to speak to?
   c. What is the purpose of his call?
   d. Why can Ralf's boss not contact the caller until the 15th of the month?
4. Find out the following technical information about the vehicle in question:
   a. the engine size
   b. the top speed
   c. the distance that can be travelled on a single charge.

After watching

5. Use the information in parts 3 and 4 to write a short memo for Ralf's boss explaining who called and what the call was about, and giving other key information.
6. How does Ralf handle the phone call? Discuss what he did well and what he could improve.

V3 Job interview

lingua tv – we watch languages!

Before watching

1. Describe the photo.

While watching

2. Write down three of the questions that the interviewer asks.
3. Watch the film again and answer the questions.
   a. What is the applicant's name?
   b. What position is he applying for?
   c. What position did the applicant hold in his last job?
   d. According to the applicant, what is his greatest strength?
   e. What is the applicant's weakness?
   f. What questions does the applicant ask the interviewer?

After watching

4. Do you think the applicant will get the job? Give reasons for your answer.

V4 Technical support

lingua tv – we watch languages!

While watching

1. What does 'rebooting the system' mean?
2. Watch the video again and decide whether the following statements are true or false.
   a. The caller cannot connect to the Internet.
   b. He has been having problems for two days now.
   c. He has tried rebooting the system.
   d. Turning the modem on and off did not help the problem.
   e. The scanner is not connected to the caller's computer.
   f. The technical support employee is unable to solve the problem with the scanner.

After watching

3. Make a list of problems that employees may have with their computers.
4. Record the call by copying the headings onto a sheet of paper and filling in the information.

Name of caller • Problem(s) • Solution(s) • Further action necessary: Yes / No

V 5 Waste – the future's most valuable resource

ZDF.enterprises

Before watching

1. What things do you recycle every day, and how?
2. How many different waste bins does your city or community provide per household?

While watching

3. Watch the film and find out the following information:
   a. How many tons of rubbish does Germany produce each year?
   b. What nations are eager to pay for our rubbish?
   c. What metal is particularly desirable for recycling?

4. Watch the film again and answer the following questions:
   a. How many tons of copper were stolen in Germany?
   b. How much heat can one ton of residual waste produce?

After watching

5. Explain these phrases / sentences from the film in your own words.
   a. “modern urban warfare”
   b. “Our waste is getting a second lease on life.”

V 6 Pipe inspection

ZDF.enterprises

Before watching

1. What do pipelines transport?

While watching

2. Watch the film and find out the following information:
   a. What is the inspection device called?
   b. How long is it?
   c. How fast does the device travel?
   d. How many days does it take to inspect 300 km of pipeline?

3. Watch the film again and answer the following questions:
   a. Where are the data analyzed?
   b. How accurate is the data grid?
   c. What does the device use to identify defects?

After watching

4. What may cause defects in or damage to pipelines?

V7 High voltage work

ZDF.enterprises

Before watching

1. What do you think the men in the steel basket are preparing to do?

While watching

2. Watch the film and find out the following:
   a. what weather conditions are necessary for repairing overhead power lines.
   b. how many volts of electricity high-voltage lines carry.
   c. how the repairmen get to the damaged lines.
   d. what safety measures are taken.

3. Watch the film again and answer the following questions:
   a. How long does the job shown in the film take?
   b. Where is the electricity switched off and on?

After watching

4. Why is it important that the men work quickly?
5. Explain in your own words: "A power cut can quickly bring an entire city to its knees."

V8 Ras Laffan

ZDF.enterprises

While watching

1. Watch the film and find out the following:
   a. where Ras Laffan is located.
   b. what is processed there.
   c. how much is processed each year.
   d. how large the Ras Laffan industrial region is.

2. Watch the film again and answer the following:
   a. What problems do the construction workers face?
   b. How is the concrete cooled, and why?
   c. Why is the gas cooled?

After watching

3. Explain the phrase "liquid gold".

V9 Pipelines

ZDF.enterprises

Before watching

1. Name some things which are transported in pipelines.

While watching

2. Watch the film and find out the following:
   a. what alloy is popular for making long-distance pipelines.
   b. how thick are the steel plates that are formed into round pipes.
   c. the welding technique used in the factory shown.
   d. what the expander is for.

3. Watch the film again and answer the following:
   a. What conditions do offshore pipelines have to cope with?
   b. Why do they have an additional outer casing of concrete?

After watching

4. Explain why quality-control checks are important in the production of pipelines.

V10 Robots in the hospital

ZDF.enterprises

While watching

1. Watch the film and find out the following:
   a. What hospital is shown as an example? Which parts of the hospital do we see?
   b. How many robots do they have?
   c. What powers the robot couriers and how do they navigate?
   d. What is a 'lift-and-tunnel system'?

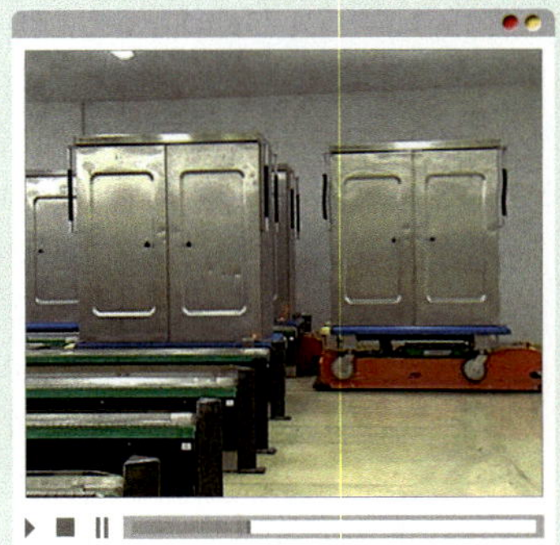

2. Watch the film again and answer these questions:
   a. What metal in the plates keeps the food warm?
   b. Do the robots distribute the food to the patients?
   c. How many containers are used to transport food?
   d. How does the hospital director feel about using robots to transport patients?

After watching

3. What else do you think the robots transport in the hospital?
4. Where else might transportation robots be used?

V11 Portable power stations

BBC Motion Gallery

Before watching

1. Think of situations in which a portable power station like the one in the photo could be useful.

While watching

2. Watch the film and list the uses of electrical power 'out in the open' that the reporter mentions.

3. Watch the film again and answer the following:
   a. What supplies the power for the 12-volt portable power station?
   b. Why are batteries not such a good choice?
   c. Where was the portable power station invented?

After watching

4. Do you think the inventor will be able to sell his power station in Germany? Where might the need for it be greater?

V12 Car speed control

BBC Motion Gallery

Before watching

1. What speed limit is acceptable
   a. on city streets?
   b. on the motorway?

While watching

2. Watch the film and find out the following:
   a. how many people die in road accidents in the UK every year.
   b. what the MIRA is working on.
   c. what the satellite positioning system does.

3. Watch the film again and answer the following:
   a. Is speed control popular with car manufacturers? Why or why not?
   b. Do speed cameras have any effect on driving habits?
   c. How is the speed-control system being tested?

After watching

4. Would you buy a car with a speed-control system? Give reasons for your answer.

KMK-Prüfungssätze

KMK Stufe I *(100 VP)*

1 Rezeption (Hörverstehen) — **20 VP**

⊙ A 6.1 **Sie interessieren sich für eine Stelle im englischsprachigen Ausland, z. B. ein Praktikum oder eine längerfristige Anstellung nach der Gesellen- oder Facharbeiterprüfung. Die Virtual Employment Agency (VEA) vermittelt solche Praktika. Sie laden einen Podcast mit vier Stellenangeboten herunter. Erstellen Sie hierzu eine Tabelle mit folgenden Stichwörtern und hören Sie den Podcast zweimal an. Füllen Sie Ihre Tabelle auf Englisch aus.**

Information number	1 *(5 VP)*	2 *(5 VP)*	3 *(5 VP)*	4 *(5 VP)*
trade / position offered				
length of practical				
company and location of practical				
requirements				
extra information: email address, telephone number if given				

2 Rezeption (Leseverstehen) — **20 VP**

Sie möchten Ihren Arbeitgeber überzeugen, Sie während Ihrer Ausbildung für ein Praktikum im Ausland freizustellen und haben dazu folgendes Informationsmaterial von der Internetseite der VEA heruntergeladen. Ihr Arbeitgeber bittet Sie, folgende Fragen zu diesem Text auf Deutsch zu beantworten.

1. Was erfahren wir über die Organisation der VEA? *(2 VP)*
2. Welche Vorteile eines Praktikums werden genannt? *(3 VP)*
3. Was konkret bietet die VEA an? *(3 VP)*
4. Was wird über eine Bezahlung / einen Kostenzuschuss für die Praktikanten gesagt? *(3 VP)*
5. Wie lange dauern die angebotenen Praktika? *(3 VP)*
6. Wer kann sich bei der VEA bewerben und welche Voraussetzungen sollten die Bewerber mitbringen? *(3 VP)*
7. Wie bewirbt man sich? Welche Unterlagen müssen geschickt werden? *(3 VP)*

London-based VEA offers job placements

Who we are

VEA is an organisation funded by the European Union and European companies. Our aim is to help to make European companies fit to operate more effectively in a global world by giving their trainees a chance to work abroad, improve their English language skills and become acquainted with a new culture. The trainees who take part in the programme have a chance to see different work techniques and learn to adapt to new working conditions.

▶

What we offer
VEA helps trainees to find work placements in England, Scotland and Wales. We have lists of companies in all kinds of trades who offer work placements. All placements take place in an authentic work environment. We can help you to establish contacts with companies and to plan your stay. We have a telephone hotline if problems should come up.
What payment is given
VEA does not pay trainees any money for the work placement, but we can pay a fixed amount towards your travelling expenses. However, most of the companies that we have under contract offer small salaries that will enable you to cover daily expenses such as food and board.
How long do work placements last?
The duration of work placements depends on the companies. Placements usually last between eight and ten weeks, but most companies are flexible if you want to arrange different periods. The shortest possible placement is three weeks.
Who can apply
All trainees can apply after their first or second year of training. The applicants should have a fair working knowledge of English. They should be communicative, interested in our culture and willing to participate in social activities if these are offered by the company.
How to apply
Send an email and a CV as an attachment in English telling us why you would like to take part in our work placement programme. You should also send written consent and a letter of recommendation from your company. And don't forget to mention the dates you would like to do the placement and the trade you would like to work in. Send your application by email to info@vea...biz subject matter "work placement."

(363 words)

3 Produktion **30 VP**

Sie wollen sich per E-Mail bei der VEA um ein Praktikum bewerben (Adresse: info@ vea...biz). Schreiben Sie, dass Ihre Firma es lieber hätte, wenn Sie zunächst einmal nur drei Wochen auf ein Auslandspraktikum gingen. Geben Sie an, welchen Beruf Sie lernen und in welchem Jahr Ihrer Ausbildung Sie sich befinden. Nennen Sie einen Zeitraum von drei Wochen (mit genauem Datum), in dem Sie ein Praktikum machen möchten.

4 Mediation **30 VP**

Auf der Internetseite befinden sich auch Erfahrungsberichte früherer Absolventen. Einer hat Ihnen besonders gefallen. Sie übertragen ihn ins Deutsche, um ihn ebenfalls Ihrem Arbeitgeber vorzulegen. Auf eine wörtliche Übersetzung legt er keinen Wert, lediglich auf eine inhaltlich korrekte Wiedergabe.

My name is Michael. I'm in my third year of training as a car mechanic. I've just come back from a three-month placement in South Wales. It was sponsored by the Leonardo Programme. My company in Germany ▶

encouraged me to apply for the placement. They even sponsored me by paying my wages even though I wasn't working for them for three months.
I worked in a company based near Cardiff that makes parts for the automobile industry. First I spent a few days in each department of the company, and then I was fully involved in the production process.
I worked with a Welsh colleague in the CNC centre. Of course I had some experience with CNC from my own company. I must say, I learned a lot, especially how to work more efficiently and independently.
In the beginning the language was a bit of a problem, but after a couple of weeks we managed to communicate quite well, and I learned many technical words and phrases.
This placement was a great opportunity for me, and my boss sees it as a real plus for our company and our business with British customers.

(193 words)

KMK Stufe II *(100 VP)*

1 Rezeption (Hörverstehen) — 8 VP

◎ A 6.2

Ihre Firma stellt Hydraulikaggregate her. Sie werden gebeten, eine Nachricht auf dem Anrufbeantworter Ihrer Firma abzuhören und eine kurze Telefonnotiz auf Deutsch zu erstellen.
Bevor Sie die Nachricht abhören, bereiten Sie auf einem Blatt eine Telefonnotiz mit folgenden Überschriften vor.

1. Name des Anrufers und der Firma *(2 VP)*
2. Sitz der Firma *(1 VP)*
3. Nachricht für … *(1 VP)*
4. Grund des Anrufes *(2 VP)*
5. Auftragsnummer *(1 VP)*
6. Rückrufnummer *(1 VP)*

2 Rezeption (Hörverstehen) — 12 VP

◎ A 6.3

Für die Herstellung von Steuerungen und Motoren sind seltene Erden unverzichtbar. Ihr Ausbildungsleiter hat zu seltenen Erden einen englischen Podcast gefunden. Da der Ausbilder nicht so gut Englisch kann, bittet er Sie, sich den Podcast anzuhören und folgende Fragen auf Deutsch zu beantworten.

1. Was wird über den Bedarf an seltenen Erden in der Einführung gesagt? *(1 VP)*
2. Welche Hinweise werden in der Einführung über die Rolle Chinas gegeben? *(2 VP)*
3. Ihr Ausbildungsleiter hat nicht genau verstanden, ob und wie seltene Erden wiederverwertet werden können. Notieren Sie die Aussage des Sprechers auf Deutsch. *(1 VP)*
4. Der Podcast nennt einige Bereiche, in denen seltene Erden unverzichtbar sind. Nennen Sie vier dieser Bereiche. *(2 VP)*
5. In welchem Bereich werden gleich mehrere Kilogramm an seltenen Erden pro Einheit gebraucht? *(1 VP)*

6. Wie selten sind seltene Erden nach Auskunft des Podcasts wirklich? *(1 VP)*
7. Es werden Produktionszahlen für China genannt: Wie hoch ist der Anteil der Chinesen an den geschätzten Reserven weltweit? *(1 VP)*
8. Welche anderen Länder werden genannt, in denen seltene Erden gefördert werden? *(2 VP)*
9. Welche Sorgen plagen das amerikanische Repräsentantenhaus? *(1 VP)*

3 **Rezeption (Leseverstehen)** 20 VP

Im Umgang mit Druckluft müssen bestimmte Sicherheitsregeln beherzigt werden. Bei einem Druckluftwerkzeug, das Ihre Firma geliefert bekam, war folgendes Faltblatt beigefügt. Ihr Ausbilder stellt Ihnen dazu ein paar Fragen, die Sie anhand dieses Textes auf Deutsch auf einem gesonderten Blatt beantworten sollen.

1. Der Text zählt eine Reihe von Druckluftwerkzeugen auf. Nennen Sie acht davon in der Reihenfolge, in der der Text sie aufführt. *(4 VP)*
2. Welche Sicherheitsausrüstung muss laut Text benutzt werden? *(2 VP)*
3. Was muss zum Schutz Ihrer Mitarbeiter getan werden? *(2 VP)*
4. Wie sind laut Text Druckluftwerkzeuge zu behandeln? *(3 VP)*
5. Was wird über die Zusatzgeräte ausgesagt? *(1 VP)*
6. Welche allgemeinen Eigenschaften sollen die Schläuche haben (bitte in der Reihenfolge aufführen wie im Text)? *(2 VP)*
7. Welche speziellen Eigenschaften hinsichtlich des Druckes sind bei den Schläuchen einzuhalten? *(2 VP)*
8. Was müssen Sie laut Text tun, bevor Sie Werkzeuge an den Druckluftschlauch anschließen? *(1 VP)*
9. Welchen Anforderungen müssen die Schlauchverbindungen entsprechen? *(2 VP)*
10. Druckluft wird gerne auch zur Reinigung verwendet. Was wird über die Reinigung mit Druckluft in diesem Text ausgesagt? *(1 VP)*

What are pneumatic tools?

- Pneumatic tools are powered by compressed air. Common types of these air-powered hand tools that are used in industry include buffers, nailing and stapling guns, grinders, drills, jack hammers, chipping hammers, riveting guns, sanders and wrenches.

How do you use pneumatic tools safely?

- Review the manufacturer's instruction before using a tool.
- Wear safety glasses or goggles, or a face shield and, where necessary, safety shoes or boots and hearing protection.
- Post warning signs where pneumatic tools are used. Set up screens or shields in areas where nearby workers may be exposed to flying fragments, chips, dust, and excessive noise.
- Ensure that the compressed air supplied to the tool is clean and dry. Dust, moisture, and corrosive fumes can damage a tool. An in-line regulator filter and lubricator increases tool life.
- Keep tools clean and lubricated, and maintain them according to the manufacturer's instructions.

▶

- Use only the attachments that the manufacturer recommends for the tools you are using.
- Be careful to prevent hands, feet, or body from injury in case the machine slips or the tool breaks.
- Reduce physical fatigue by supporting heavy tools with a counter-balance wherever possible.

How should you handle air hoses?

- Use the proper hose and fittings of the correct diameter.
- Use hoses specifically designed to resist abrasion, cutting, crushing and failure from continuous flexing.
- Choose air-supply hoses that have a minimum working pressure rating of 1035 kPa (150 psig) or 150% of the maximum pressure produced in the system, whichever is higher.
- Check hoses regularly for cuts, bulges and abrasions. Tag and replace, if defective.
- Blow out the air line before connecting a tool. Hold hose firmly and blow away from yourself and others.
- Make sure that hose connections fit properly and are equipped with a mechanical means of securing the connection (e.g. chain, wire, or positive locking device).
- Install quick disconnects of a pressure-release type rather than a disengagement type. Attach the male end of the connector to the tool, NOT the hose.
- Do not operate the tool at a pressure above the manufacturer's rating.
- Turn off the air pressure to hose when not in use or when changing power tools.
- Do not carry a pneumatic tool by its hose.
- Avoid creating trip hazards caused by hoses laid across walkways or curled underfoot.
- Do not use compressed air to blow debris or to clean dirt from clothes.

What should you avoid with compressed air?

- Cleaning with compressed air is dangerous.
- Do not use compressed air for cleaning unless no alternate method of cleaning is available. The nozzle pressure MUST remain below 207 kPa (30 psi). Personal protective equipment and effective chip guarding techniques must be used. (…)

(489 words)

4 Mediation **30 VP**

Im Lernfeldunterricht Ihrer Berufsschule bekommen Sie folgenden (siehe nächste Seite) englischen Text vorgelegt. Lesen Sie ihn durch und übertragen Sie die wichtigsten Punkte in zusammenhängenden Sätzen ins Deutsche. Eine wörtliche Übersetzung ist nicht gewünscht.

Processes for joining metals

When metals are to be joined different processes can be applied such as welding, soldering and brazing. There are two kinds of welding: gas welding and electric-arc welding. By definition, welding is a fusion process that joins materials of the same kind, usually metals or thermoplastics. This is often done by melting the workpieces and adding a filler to form a pool of molten material that cools to become a strong joint; pressure is sometimes used together with high temperature, up to 3000°C, to produce the weld.

This is in contrast to soldering and brazing, which use a material with a lower melting point between the workpieces to form a bond between them without melting the workpieces.

The solder used in soldering has a melting point of up to 450°C. The parts which are to be joined are heated, and the solder is pressed against them. The solder melts and flows into the joint. After the material has cooled down, the joint is finished.

Higher temperatures are needed in brazing: the solder has a melting point of between 450°C and 900°C. Metals suitable for brazing are steel, copper, silver and brass.

Electrical engineers apply soldering to join electronic parts onto a PCB (printed circuit board), for example. Plumbers use this joining technique to fit water or gas pipes, to join drain pipes or gutters, or to generate roof sealings.

(233 words)

5 Produktion **30 VP**

Ihre Firma plant einen Messeauftritt auf der *Automotive Testing Expo* in Shanghai. Zur Vorbereitung hatte sie zwei Monate vor dem Messetermin den Besuch eines Mitarbeiters in Shanghai geplant, um mit chinesischen Zulieferern den Auftritt zu besprechen. Leider wurde der Termin von chinesischer Seite kurzfristig um zwei Wochen verschoben. Schreiben Sie eine E-Mail mit folgenden Punkten an das Royal Victoria Hotel in Shanghai info@royalvictoria . . . com .

- Bedanken Sie sich für die Reservierung eines Einzelzimmers mit Dusche, Satellitenfernseher, schnurlosem Telefon und Internetanschluss für Nichtraucher sowie für die Reservierung eines Sitzungsraumes für kurze Geschäftsbesprechungen für den Zeitraum 01.–08.08.20...
- Teilen Sie mit, dass Sie die Reservierungen leider stornieren müssen, weil Ihre Geschäftsreise um zwei Wochen verschoben werden musste.
- Fragen Sie an, ob Sie Ihre Buchungen ebenfalls um zwei Wochen verschieben können, und zwar auf den 15.–22.08... .
- Bitten Sie um eine schriftliche Bestätigung der neuen Buchungen.
- Bitten Sie um die Empfehlung eines anderen Hotels für den Fall, dass das Royal Victoria Hotel zu dem gewünschten Termin keine Zimmer mehr frei hat.
- Denken Sie beim Verfassen Ihrer E-Mail auch an die äußere Form der E-Mail wie Betreff, Anrede, Schluss und Grußformel.

Role cards

Module C Telephoning, B 3

→ **PHRASES:** Telephoning

Partner A

Give your partner the following information:

1. The room is 54 m^2.
2. The wire needs to be 128.5 cm long.
3. The doors are 80 cm x 220 cm.
4. Each of the components weighs around 0.75 kg.

Module 4 Picking and consigning goods, 2

Partner B

Use the picking list below. Ask your partner for the missing information and complete your picking list.

Sold to: 1
Ship to: Weidner AG
Zentrales Auslieferungslager
Bahnhofstraße 12
38100 Braunschweig
Item no.: 2
Description: car radios
Account no.: 3

Salesperson no.: 05
Order no.: 4
Date shipped: 23 May 20…
Quantity ordered: 5 ; **shipped:** 200
Terms: 6
Storage area: B 38/04-01526

Module 5 Packing goods, A 5

→ **PHRASES:** Meeting people

Partner A: Lagerleiter(in)

- Begrüßen Sie die/den Auszubildende(n).
- Fragen Sie, was sie/ihn während des Aufenthalts besonders beeindruckt hat.
- Bitten Sie um eine Erklärung, worauf beim Versand zerbrechlicher Güter geachtet werden muss.
- Fragen Sie, warum heutzutage die Verpackung von Produkten eine wesentlich größere Rolle spielt als früher.
- Erläutern Sie die Vorteile einheitlicher Verpackungsgrößen mit Bezug auf die Lagerung und den Warentransport.
- Wünschen Sie dem/der Auszubildenden eine gute Heimreise und verabschieden Sie sich.

Module C Telephoning, B 3

→ **PHRASES:** Telephoning

Partner B

Give your partner the following information:

1. The table is 2 m x 3 m.
2. The engine runs at 7500 rpm.
3. 220 V sockets are standard in Germany.
4. The customer would like the work surface to be 24 mm thick.

Module 5 Packing goods, A 5

→ **PHRASES:** Meeting people

Partner B: Auszubildende(n)

- Begrüßen Sie den/die Lagerleiter(in) und sagen Sie, dass Ihnen die Arbeit Spaß gemacht hat und Sie viel gelernt haben.
- Erwidern Sie, dass Sie überrascht waren, dass es so viele unterschiedliche Verpackungsarten gibt.
- Beantworten Sie die Frage, indem Sie auf die Kennzeichnung der Verpackung eingehen und die Konsequenzen erläutern, wenn diese unterbleibt.
- Geben Sie eine passende Antwort und fragen Sie, warum es überwiegend einheitliche Verpackungsgrößen gibt.
- Bedanken Sie sich für den angenehmen Aufenthalt und verabschieden Sie sich angemessen.

Module 7 Shipping goods, C 2

Read the information and use a dictionary if necessary. Then choose three Incoterms and take turns asking your partner what they mean and who bears what risks and costs during transport.

Incoterms 2020

Incoterms are national and international rules that define how the tasks, costs and risks during the transportation of goods are divided between the seller and the buyer. There are two categories of Incoterms:
- rules for any mode(s) of transport
- rules only for sea and inland waterway transport.

▶

Any mode(s) of transport:

EXW (Ex Works) = Ab Werk: The seller prepares the goods for collection at his or her location (for example, the factory or warehouse) and the buyer picks them up there. The buyer takes over the risk for the goods at the seller's location when he or she picks them up.
FCA (Free Carrier) = Frei Frachtführer: The buyer chooses a carrier and the seller delivers the goods to the carrier. The buyer bears the risk from the point when the goods are handed over to the carrier.
CPT (Carriage Paid to) = Frachtfrei: The seller delivers the goods to a carrier chosen by him or her and pays the transport costs to the specified destination. The buyer bears the risk for the goods from the point when the goods are handed over to the carrier.
CIP (Carriage and Insurance Paid to) = Frachtfrei versichert: The seller delivers the goods to a carrier chosen by him or her and pays the costs for transport and insurance to the specified destination. The buyer bears the risk for the goods from the point when the goods are handed over to the carrier.
DPU (Delivered at Place unloaded) = Geliefert benannter Ort entladen: The seller places the goods of the buyer's disposal, unloaded, at the named place of destination. The buyer bears the risk when the goods have been unloaded at the place of destination.
DAP (Delivered at Place) = Geliefert benannter Ort: The seller delivers the goods to the destination specified by the buyer, ready for unloading. The buyer takes over the risk for the goods, still unloaded, at the specified destination.
DDP (Delivered Duty Paid) = Geliefert verzollt: The seller delivers the goods to the destination specified by the buyer, ready for unloading, and carries out all customs formalities (including payment of import duty), if necessary. The buyer takes over the risk for the goods, still unloaded, at the specified destination.

Sea and inland waterway transport:

FAS (Free alongside Ship) = Frei Längsseite Schiff: The seller delivers the goods alongside the ship at the port of shipment specified by the buyer. The buyer bears the risk for the goods from the moment when they are placed alongside the ship ready for loading.
FOB (Free on Board) = Frei an Bord: The seller delivers the goods on board the ship at the port of shipment specified by the buyer. The buyer bears the risk for the goods from the point when they are on board the ship.
CFR (Cost and Freight) = Kosten und Fracht: The seller delivers the goods on board the ship and pays the cost and freight to the port of destination specified by the buyer. The buyer bears the risk for the goods from the point when they are on board the ship.
CIF (Cost, Insurance and Freight) = Kosten, Versicherung und Fracht: The seller delivers the goods on board the ship and pays the cost and freight to the port of destination and the insurance for the goods during transportation. The buyer bears the risk for the goods from the point when they are on board the ship.

Phrases

A | Meeting people

Formal greetings	Formelle Begrüßung
Good morning / afternoon / evening, Ms Robinson / Mr Jones.	Guten Morgen / Tag / Abend, Frau Robinson / Herr Jones.
Good morning / afternoon / evening, ladies and gentlemen.	Guten Morgen / Tag / Abend, meine Damen und Herren.
Informal greetings	**Informelle Begrüßung**
Good morning, Susan / James.	Guten Morgen, Susan / James.
Hi / Hello / Morning, Karl.	Tag / Morgen, Karl.
Hi everybody!	Tag zusammen!
Formal goodbyes	**Formelle Verabschiedung**
Goodbye! It's been nice / pleasant meeting you.	Auf Wiedersehen! Es war nett / angenehm, Sie kennen zu lernen!
Thank you for your help / your time. Let's keep in touch.	Danke für Ihre Hilfe / Ihre Zeit. Wir bleiben in Kontakt.
Informal goodbyes	**Informelle Verabschiedung**
Bye!	Tschüss / Ciao!
See you later!	Bis später!
See you around!	Wir sehen uns!
See you tomorrow / on Monday / next week!	Bis morgen / Montag / nächste Woche!
Formal introduction	**Formelle Vorstellung**
May I introduce myself?	Darf ich mich vorstellen?
Hello, my name is / I'm Lukas Hansen from ATW Shipping.	Hallo, mein Name ist / ich heiße Lukas Hansen von ATW Shipping.
Pleased to meet you. / Nice to meet you. / How do you do?	Angenehm. / Sehr erfreut.
It's a pleasure to finally meet you in person.	Es freut mich sehr, Sie endlich einmal persönlich kennen zu lernen.
Informal introduction	**Informelle Vorstellung**
Hi. I'm Peter, Peter James.	Hi. Ich bin Peter, Peter James.
Hello, my name is Sarah O'Neill.	Hallo, ich heiße Sarah O'Neill.
Hi Sarah. Nice to meet you.	Hi Sarah. Freut mich, dich kennen zu lernen.

Introducing others (formal)	Andere miteinander bekannt machen (formell)
Have you met our managing director?	Haben Sie schon unsere Geschäftsführerin / unseren Geschäftsführer kennen gelernt?
Ms Hall? May I introduce you to Christian Eriksen, our new intern? Christian, Georgina Hall from our sales department.	Frau Hall? Darf ich Sie Christian Eriksen, unserem neuen Praktikanten, vorstellen? Christian, das ist Georgina Hall von unserer Verkaufsabteilung.
Introducing others (informal)	**Andere miteinander bekannt machen (informell)**
Here's someone I'd like you to meet.	Ich möchte euch gerne jemanden vorstellen.
Christian, this is Joe. Joe, Christian.	Christian, das ist Joe. Joe, das ist Christian.
Let me introduce you to the team.	Darf ich dich dem Team vorstellen?
Use of first names	**Verwendung von Vornamen**
Please call me Martin.	Bitte nennen Sie mich ruhig Martin.
My name's Marianne.	Ich heiße Marianne.
My first name's Andrew, but everybody calls me Andy.	Mein Vorname ist Andrew, aber alle nennen mich Andy.
May I call you Anna?	Darf ich Anna zu Ihnen sagen?

B | Your company

Introducing the company	Die Firma vorstellen
Our company was founded in 1997.	Unsere Firma wurde 1997 gegründet.
In 2005 we were taken over by ...	2005 wurden wir von ... übernommen.
We are a leading manufacturer of engines.	Wir sind ein führender Hersteller von Motoren.
We are a medium-sized family firm.	Wir sind ein mittelständisches Familienunternehmen.
We are a manufacturer of industrial cleaning machines specializing in high-pressure cleaners.	Wir sind ein Hersteller von industriellen Reinigungsgeräten und sind auf Hochdruckreiniger spezialisiert.
I work for a major construction company.	Ich arbeite bei einem bedeutenden Bauunternehmen.
We are a subsidiary of ...	Wir sind eine Tochtergesellschaft von ...
We are a chain of electronics suppliers.	Wir sind eine Kette von Elektronik-Anbietern.
Describing the company's products / services	**Die Produkte / Dienstleistungen der Firma beschreiben**
We offer sustainable solutions.	Wir bieten nachhaltige Lösungen an.
Our products are environmentally friendly.	Unsere Produkte sind umweltfreundlich.
Our products are well-known in Europe.	Unsere Produkte sind europaweit bekannt.
Our components are both reliable and long-lasting.	Unsere Komponenten sind zuverlässig und haben eine lange Lebensdauer.
Our software is adapted to suit your requirements.	Unsere Software wird Ihren Bedürfnissen angepasst.
We manufacture high-tech shock absorbers.	Wir stellen High-Tech-Stoßdämpfer her.
Our products are designed using the latest CAD technology.	Unsere Produkte werden mit der neuesten CAD-Technologie entworfen.

Describing the job	Den Beruf beschreiben
I'm training to become a …	Ich mache eine Lehre / Ausbildung zur / zum …
I am a bricklayer / carpenter / technician / plumber / joiner.	Ich bin Maurer(in), Zimmermann / Zimmerin, Techniker(in), Klempner(in), Schreiner(in).
I work in the automotive industry.	Ich arbeite in der Automobilindustrie.
I work with automated machines.	Ich arbeite mit automatisierten Maschinen.
Describing the workplace	**Den Arbeitsplatz beschreiben**
I work on an assembly line / a machine.	Ich arbeite am Fließband / an einer Maschine.
I work in a large warehouse / factory.	Ich arbeite in einem großen Warenlager / einer großen Fabrik.
I work in a garage / workshop.	Ich arbeite in einer Autowerkstatt / Werkstatt.
I work on a building site.	Ich arbeite auf einer Baustelle.
Talking about tasks and responsibilities	**Über Aufgaben und Zuständigkeiten sprechen**
I am responsible for programming the machines.	Ich bin für die Programmierung der Maschinen zuständig.
I report to the foreman.	Ich bin dem Meister / Vorarbeiter unterstellt.
I work shifts.	Ich mache Schichtarbeit.
I often have to do overtime.	Ich muss oft Überstunden machen.
I repair electrical devices.	Ich repariere elektrische Geräte.

C | Telephoning

1. Answering the phone	Sich am Telefon melden
Introducing yourself	**Sich vorstellen**
Smart EDV GmbH, good morning. Hendrik Klopp speaking.	Smart EDV GmbH, guten Morgen. Hendrik Klopp am Apparat.
Offering help	**Hilfe anbieten**
How may I help you? / Can I help you?	(Wie) kann ich Ihnen helfen?
What can I do for you?	Was kann ich für Sie tun?
Asking for details	**Nach Details fragen**
Who's calling, please?	Wer ist am Apparat, bitte?
May I / Can I ask who's calling, please?	Darf ich fragen, wer anruft?
May I / can I take your name, please?	Könnten Sie mir bitte Ihren Namen nennen?
Could you spell that please?	Könnten Sie das bitte buchstabieren?

Connecting	Verbinden
One moment, please. I'm putting you through now.	Einen Moment bitte, ich verbinde Sie.
Shall I put you through to …?	Soll ich Sie mit … verbinden?
Hold the line, please. I'll put you through.	Bitte bleiben Sie am Apparat. Ich verbinde.
Your boss is not available	**Der / die Vorgesetzte ist nicht zu sprechen**
I'm afraid Mr Deschler is not in the office at the moment.	Es tut mir leid, Herr Deschler ist z. Zt. leider nicht in seinem Büro.
… He is on a building site.	… Er ist auf einer Baustelle.
… He has a visitor with him.	… Er hat Besuch.
… He is out at lunch.	… Er ist in der Mittagspause.
Offering to call back	**Einen Rückruf anbieten**
Shall I ask her to call you back?	Soll ich sie bitten, Sie zurückzurufen?
Can she call you back this afternoon?	Kann sie Sie heute Nachmittag zurückrufen?
Does he have your telephone number?	Hat er Ihre Telefonnummer?
Can I just confirm your number?	Kann ich Ihre Nummer nochmals überprüfen?
I'll just repeat that.	Ich wiederhole.
Taking a message	**Eine Nachricht aufnehmen**
Can I take a message?	Kann ich etwas ausrichten?
Can I give him a message?	Kann ich ihm etwas ausrichten?
Would you like to leave a message?	Möchten Sie eine Nachricht hinterlassen?
Can I just confirm that?	Kann ich das kurz überprüfen?
So that's twenty-four square metres, isn't it?	Das sind also vierundzwanzig Quadratmeter, oder?
I'll make sure he gets the message.	Ich werde mich darum kümmern, dass er die Nachricht bekommt.
I'll tell her as soon as she comes back.	Ich sage ihr Bescheid, sobald sie zurückkommt.
Problems	**Probleme**
Sorry, I didn't quite catch that. Could you repeat it more slowly, please?	Es tut mir leid, das habe ich nicht verstanden. Könnten Sie es bitte etwas langsamer wiederholen?
I'm afraid I didn't catch the telephone number. Could you repeat it, please?	Leider habe ich die Telefonnummer nicht mitbekommen. Würden Sie sie bitte wiederholen?
I'm sorry, but we are having a bad connection. Could you repeat that, please?	Es tut mir leid, aber die Verbindung ist schlecht. Könnten Sie das bitte nochmals wiederholen?
Ending the call	**Das Telefongespräch beenden**
You're welcome.	Bitteschön. / Gern geschehen.
Thanks for calling.	Vielen Dank für Ihren Anruf.
Goodbye.	Auf Wiederhören.

2. Making a call	Jemanden anrufen
Introducing yourself	**Sich vorstellen**
This is ... from Fertighaus Henke.	Hier spricht ... von Fertighaus Henke.
My name's ... I'm calling from Smart EDV.	Mein Name ist .... Ich rufe von der Firma Smart EDV an.
Asking to speak to somebody	**Nach jemandem fragen**
Could I speak to Ms Sheringham, please?	Könnte ich bitte Frau Sheringham sprechen?
Could you put me through to Mr Ferguson?	Könnten Sie mich mit Herrn Ferguson verbinden?
Could you give me his / her extension number, please?	Könnten Sie mir bitte seine / ihre Durchwahl geben?
I'd like to speak to someone from the production planning department.	Ich möchte mit jemandem in der Fertigungsplanung sprechen.
Spelling your name	**Den Namen buchstabieren**
It's S-C-H-N-E-I-D-E-R. Schneider.	Das ist S-C-H-N-E-I-D-E-R. Schneider.
Giving your phone number	**Die Telefonnummer nennen**
It's 0049 for Germany, then 391 458 547.	Das ist die 0049 für Deutschland, dann 391 458 547.
It's 0391 458 547.	Das ist die 0391 458 547.
Leaving a message	**Eine Nachricht hinterlassen**
Yes, please. Could you tell him that ...?	Ja bitte. Könnten Sie ihm ausrichten, dass ...?
Thank you. I'll ring back later.	Danke sehr. Ich rufe später zurück.
I'm afraid I won't be in the workshop this afternoon. I'll give you my mobile number.	Leider bin ich heute Nachmittag nicht in der Werkstatt. Ich gebe Ihnen meine Handynummer.
Ending the call	**Das Telefongespräch beenden**
Thank you very much for your help.	Vielen Dank für Ihre Hilfe.
Goodbye.	Auf Wiederhören.

D | Written communication

Salutation	Anrede
Dear Sir or Madam	Sehr geehrte Damen und Herren
Dear Mr ... / Dear Ms ...	Lieber Herr ... / Liebe Frau ...
Dear Peter	Lieber Peter
Complimentary close	**Schlussformel**
Yours sincerely / Yours faithfully (rarely used)	Mit freundlichen Grüßen / Hochachtungsvoll (selten benutzt)
Best regards / Kind regards / Best wishes	Schöne Grüße / Herzliche Grüße

Enquiries	Anfragen
We have visited your website and ...	Wir haben Ihre Webseite besucht und ...
Your services have been recommended to us by ...	Ihre Dienstleistungen wurden uns von ... empfohlen.
We are a well-established manufacturer of ...	Wir sind ein gut etablierter Hersteller von ...
Our firm is a leading importer of ...	Unsere Firma ist ein führender Importeur von ...
Could you please let us have a brochure and a price list?	Wir bitten um einen Prospekt und eine Preisliste.
Please send us a quotation for ...	Bitte machen Sie uns ein Angebot über ...
Please quote your lowest prices for ...	Bitte nennen Sie uns Ihre günstigsten Preise für ...
We would be grateful for information on your terms of payment and delivery.	Wir bitten um nähere Angaben zu Ihren Liefer- und Zahlungsbedingungen.
A visit by your representative would be appreciated.	Wir wären dankbar für einen Besuch Ihres Vertreters.
We look forward to hearing from you.	Wir freuen uns darauf, bald von Ihnen zu hören.
Offers	**Angebote**
Many thanks for your enquiry of 30 May about our new range of ...	Wir danken Ihnen vielmals für Ihre Anfrage vom 30. Mai wegen unseres neuen Sortiments von ...
As requested, we are sending you enclosed our latest catalogue and price list.	Wie gewünscht fügen wir unseren neuesten Katalog und unsere Preisliste bei.
We can offer a 10% quantity discount on orders of at least 500 units.	Für Aufträge über mindestens 500 Stück wird 10% Mengenrabatt gewährt.
We take pleasure in submitting the following cost estimate:	Wir freuen uns, Ihnen folgenden Kostenvoranschlag zu unterbreiten:
Our usual terms of payment are: - cash with order - cash on delivery - 30 days net, 10 days 2% - by irrevocable letter of credit	Unsere üblichen Zahlungsbedingungen lauten: - Barzahlung bei Auftragserteilung - Barzahlung bei Lieferung - 30 Tage netto, 10 Tage 2% Skonto - durch unwiderrufliches und bestätigtes Akkreditiv
The delivery period is 6 weeks.	Die Lieferzeit beträgt 6 Wochen.
We look forward to welcoming you as our customers.	Wir freuen uns darauf, Sie als Kunden begrüßen zu dürfen.
Orders	**Bestellungen**
Please supply the following items on the terms stated below:	Bitte liefern Sie uns folgende Positionen zu den unten genannten Bedingungen:
As agreed, we will effect payment by bank transfer 30 days from date of invoice.	Wie vereinbart werden wir die Zahlung 30 Tage nach Rechnungsdatum per Banküberweisung vornehmen lassen.
Please note that the goods must reach us by 1 March at the latest.	Wir weisen darauf hin, dass die Ware bis spätestens 1. März hier eintreffen muss.
Please acknowledge this order promptly.	Bitte bestätigen Sie diesen Auftrag umgehend.
We look forward to receiving the goods in time and to doing further business with you.	Wir freuen uns, die Ware rechtzeitig entgegennehmen und weitere Geschäfte mit Ihnen machen zu können.

E | Applications

Mentioning the source of the advertisement	Die Quelle der Anzeige nennen
I would like to apply for the job / work placement which you advertised in the ... of ... / on the ... website.	Ich möchte mich auf die in der ... vom ... / auf der ... Website ausgeschriebenen Stelle / Praktikumsstelle bewerben.
I saw your advertisement for a ... (job / work placement) in the ... of ... / on the ... website and would like to apply for the position.	Ich habe Ihre Anzeige für eine Stelle / Praktikumsstelle in der ... vom ... / auf der ... Website gesehen und möchte mich auf die Stelle bewerben.
I am writing in response to your advertisement of ... in the ... / on the ... website for a ... (job / work placement).	Ich melde mich auf Ihre Anzeige vom ... in der ... / auf der ... Website für eine Stelle / Praktikumsstelle.
Introducing yourself	**Sich vorstellen**
I am particularly attracted to this position as ...	Ich bin an dieser Stelle besonders interessiert, weil ...
I am currently doing a one-year / two-year ... apprenticeship at a vocational college in ... (town), Germany.	Ich mache zurzeit eine ein-/zweijährige ... Ausbildung an einer berufsbildenden Schule in ..., Deutschland.
I am in the second year of an apprenticeship in ...	Ich bin im zweiten Jahr einer Ausbildung als ...
At present I am working as a ... with ... (company).	Zurzeit arbeite ich als ... bei der Firma ...
After completing my apprenticeship / At the end of the apprenticeship I will be a qualified (job title).	Nachdem ich meine Ausbildung beendet habe / Mit Abschluss meiner Ausbildung bin ich eine qualifizierte / ein qualifizierter (Berufsbezeichnung).
Talking about yourself and saying why you are a good applicant	**Über sich sprechen und begründen, warum man ein guter Bewerber / eine gute Bewerberin ist**
As you will see from my CV ...	Wie aus meinem Lebenslauf zu ersehen ist, ...
I have a good knowledge of ...	Ich verfüge über gute Kenntnisse in ...
I am motivated / reliable / hard-working / keen to learn / friendly / open / a good communicator.	Ich bin motiviert / zuverlässig / sehr fleißig / lernwillig / freundlich / aufgeschlossen / ein kommunikativer Mensch.
I have previous work experience as ...	Ich verfüge bereits über Berufserfahrung als ...
I have a wide range of interests including ...	Ich bin vielseitig interessiert, u.a. an ...
I am familiar with this kind of work, because ...	Mit dieser Tätigkeit bin ich vertraut, da ...
I would very much welcome the opportunity to work in ...	Über die Möglichkeit, in ... zu arbeiten, würde ich mich sehr freuen.
I believe that I would be a valuable / enthusiastic employee.	Ich bin überzeugt, dass ich ein(e) nützliche(r) / engagierte(r) Mitarbeiter(in) wäre.

Finishing the letter	Den Brief beenden
I hope that you will consider my application.	Ich hoffe, dass Sie meine Bewerbung in Betracht ziehen werden.
Thank you in advance for considering my application.	Ich danke Ihnen im Voraus, dass Sie meine Bewerbung in Betracht ziehen.
I look forward to hearing from you (soon).	Ich freue mich auf eine (baldige) Antwort.

F | Socialising

Ice breakers	Eisbrecher
How was your weekend? – Good, thanks. How about yours?	Wie war dein / Ihr Wochenende? – Gut, danke. Und bei dir / Ihnen?
Did you see the game last night? – Of course! It was unbelievable. What did you think about the red card / winning goal?	Hast du / Haben Sie das Spiel gestern abend gesehen? – Natürlich! Es war unglaublich. Was halten Sie von der roten Karte / vom Siegtor?
Quite cold / warm today, isn't it?	Ziemlich kalt / warm heute, oder?
I really like your watch. Where did you get it?	Ihre / deine Uhr gefällt mir wirklich gut. Woher haben Sie / hast du sie?
Did you read the story about … in the newspaper this morning?	Haben Sie heute Morgen den Bericht über … in der Zeitung gelesen?
Ah! I see you are also in need of a coffee / cup of tea.	Ah! Wie ich sehe brauchen Sie / brauchst du auch einen Kaffee / eine Tasse Tee.
Is this your first time in Germany?	Sind Sie / Bist du zum ersten Mal in Deutschland?
The food is pretty good here, isn't it? – You can say that again!	Das Essen hier ist ziemlich gut, oder? – Das können Sie / kannst du laut sagen.
Keeping the conversation going	**Das Gespräch in Gang halten**
Really? Is that right? You're joking!	Wirklich? Ist das wahr? Sie machen / du machst Scherze!
That's brilliant / hilarious / fascinating!	Das ist brilliant / sehr lustig / faszinierend!
And what happened then?	Und was passierte dann?
No, unfortunately I missed it. What happened?	Nein, leider habe ich es verpasst. Was ist passiert?
It's interesting you should say that, because …	Interessant, dass Sie das sagen, weil …
Talking about food, have you already tried the new Italian restaurant in the city centre?	Wo wir gerade über Essen sprechen: Haben Sie schon den neuen Italiener in der Innenstadt ausprobiert?
Changing the subject	**Das Thema wechseln**
I think it's best if we don't talk about politics.	Ich denke, es ist das Beste, wenn wir nicht über Politik sprechen.
If you don't mind, I'd rather not talk about that.	Wenn es Ihnen nichts ausmacht, würde ich lieber nicht darüber sprechen.
Yes … By the way, have you read …	Ja … Übrigens, haben Sie … gelesen?

Ending the conversation politely	Die Unterhaltung höflich beenden
Well, it's been good talking to you.	Nun, es war schön, mit Ihnen zu sprechen.
I suppose it's time to get back to work. See you around.	Ich denke, dass es Zeit ist, zur Arbeit zurückzukehren. Man sieht sich!
Excuse me, but I have just seen someone I need to speak to. It was nice talking to you.	Entschuldigen Sie, aber ich habe jemanden gesehen, mit dem ich sprechen muss. Es war nett, mit Ihnen zu reden.
Eating out	**Essen gehen**
Talking about preferences	**Über Vorlieben sprechen**
Do you eat meat / seafood / fish?	Essen Sie Fleisch / Meeresfrüchte / Fisch?
Do you like spicy food?	Mögen Sie scharfes Essen?
I'm a vegetarian / vegan.	Ich bin Vegetarier / Veganer.
I'm allergic to nuts.	Ich bin allergisch gegen Nüsse.
I'd prefer something light; I'm on a diet.	Ich würde etwas Leichtes bevorzugen – ich bin auf Diät.
I don't drink alcohol.	Ich trinke keinen Alkohol.
Talking about the menu	**Über die Speisekarte sprechen**
It's sweet / savoury / sour.	Es ist süß / herzhaft / sauer.
It's a starter / main dish / dessert.	Es ist ein(e) Vorspeise / Hauptgericht / Dessert.
What's in it?	Was ist da drin?
It's made of …	Es wird aus … gemacht.
It's boiled / fried / baked / roasted / filled with …	Es ist gekocht / gebraten/gebacken / geröstet / gefüllt mit …
Ordering	**Bestellen**
Are you ready to order?	Sind Sie bereit zum Bestellen?
As a starter, I'll take the … and then …	Als Vorspeise nehme ich …, und dann …
I'd like a side order of rice, please.	Ich hätte gerne (eine Portion) Reis als Beilage.
Shall we share a bottle of wine?	Sollen wir uns eine Flasche Wein teilen?
How do you like your steak? – Rare / medium / well-done, please.	Wie möchten Sie Ihr Steak? – Englisch / medium / durch, bitte.
What kind of wine / beer do you have?	Welche Weine / Biersorten haben Sie?
Talking about the food	**Über das Essen sprechen**
Enjoy your meal.	Guten Appetit!
How's your meal?	Wie ist Ihr Essen?
What's your … like?	Wie ist Ihr …?
The meat is very tender / a little tough.	Das Fleisch ist sehr zart / etwas zäh.
It's not as sweet as I expected.	Es ist nicht so süß, wie ich gedacht habe.
Excuse me, but my soup is cold.	Entschuldigen Sie, aber meine Suppe ist kalt.

Asking for the bill	Nach der Rechnung fragen
Excuse me, could we have the bill, please?	Entschuldigen Sie, könnten wir bitte die Rechnung haben?
Do you accept credit cards?	Akzeptieren Sie Kreditkarten?
This one's on me!	Das geht auf mich!
Shall we split the bill 50-50?	Sollen wir die Rechnung 50-50 teilen?

G | Presentations

Beginning the presentation	Die Präsentation beginnen
I should like to start by telling you about my company.	Zunächst möchte ich Ihnen etwas über meine Firma sagen.
My presentation will deal with ...	Meine Präsentation behandelt ...
I intend to keep my presentation as brief as possible.	Ich möchte meine Präsentation so kurz wie möglich halten.
I would welcome any questions at the end of my presentation.	Ich wäre gern bereit, etwaige Fragen am Ende meiner Präsentation zu beantworten.
The handout summarises the main points and gives an overview of the relevant figures and statistics.	Das Handout enthält die Hauptpunkte und gibt einen Überblick über die entsprechenden Zahlen und Statistiken.
Structuring the main part of your presentation	**Den Hauptteil der Präsentation strukturieren**
Now my second point is ...	Ich komme nun zu Punkt 2 ...
Thirdly, let me give you some basic statistics.	Drittens darf ich Ihnen ein paar grundlegende Statistiken zeigen.
I should now like to move on to the next topic.	Ich möchte nun gern zum nächsten Thema übergehen.
An excellent example of this is ...	Ein hervorragendes Beispiel dafür ist ...
I should like to give you an example to illustrate this point.	Ich möchte diesen Punkt mit einem Beispiel erläutern.
Concluding your presentation	**Die Präsentation beenden**
To sum up we can say that ...	Zusammenfassend kann man sagen, dass ...
I should like to finish by saying / thanking the organisers / pointing out ...	Ich möchte schließen mit der Bemerkung / dem Dank an die Organisatoren / dem Hinweis ...
Are there any questions?	Gibt es Fragen?
Thank you for your attention.	Vielen Dank für Ihre Aufmerksamkeit.

H | Dealing with customers

Making a complaint	Eine Beschwerde / Reklamation vorbringen
We are writing with reference to our order no. …	Wir nehmen Bezug auf unseren Auftrag Nr. …
On unpacking the cases our Incoming Goods Control discovered that 15 items are missing.	Beim Auspacken der Kisten stellte unsere Warenannahme fest, dass 15 Positionen fehlen.
We are afraid that several units are - seriously damaged / defective. - broken / badly scratched / stained.	Leider sind mehrere Teile - schwer beschädigt / schadhaft. - zerbrochen / stark zerkratzt / verschmutzt.
We are sorry to point out that the repair work has been poorly executed.	Wir müssen leider darauf hinweisen, dass die Reparatur schlecht ausgeführt wurde.
We believe the damage may be due to rough handling in transit.	Wir glauben, dass der Schaden auf unsachgemäße Behandlung beim Transport zurückzuführen ist.
This is very inconvenient for us because …	Dies kommt uns sehr ungelegen, da …
We would ask you to - replace the faulty goods at your expense. - grant us a price reduction of 10 %. - cut the price to € 550.	Wir möchten Sie bitten, - die mangelhafte Ware auf Ihre Kosten zu ersetzen. - uns einen Preisnachlass von 10 % zu gewähren. - den Preis auf € 550 zu senken.
We will keep the damaged goods until we hear from you.	Wir werden die beschädigten Waren behalten, bis wir von Ihnen hören.
Responding to a complaint	**Auf eine Beschwerde / Reklamation antworten**
Thank you for your email drawing a serious problem to our attention.	Danke für Ihre E-Mail, mit der Sie uns auf ein ernstes Problem aufmerksam gemacht haben.
We wish to apologise for this mistake.	Wir bitten für diesen Fehler um Entschuldigung.
We are extremely sorry for the poor service you have received.	Es tut uns außerordentlich leid, dass Sie einen unzureichenden Service erhalten haben.
We will investigate the matter thoroughly and inform you of the steps taken.	Wir werden die Angelegenheit gründlich untersuchen und Sie über die Schritte informieren, die wir unternommen haben.
Please return the faulty items at our expense.	Bitte senden Sie die mangelhaften Artikel auf unsere Kosten zurück.
We are prepared to reduce the price by 10 % if you decide to keep the goods.	Wir sind bereit, den Preis um 10 % zu senken, wenn Sie sich entschließen, die Ware zu behalten.
We hope that this proposal will find your approval.	Wir hoffen, dieser Vorschlag findet Ihre Zustimmung.

Audioscripts

A 3.16 Module 1 Receiving and checking goods, B 2, 3

Jan Kowalski: Hello Gerd. I have the goods from Gusto Coffee Machines that you've been waiting for in my truck outside.

Gerd Wolters: Hi Jan. We can start checking the documents so that the goods can be unloaded.

Jan Kowalski: That's great.

Gerd Wolters: Well, we have a receiving note for 600 coffee machines, type Meldiva, item number 143. OK, now let me have a look at the delivery note. The delivery address is correct: Paul Steiner GmbH, Am Ringbrunnen 23 in Bremen and the supplier's address is correct, too. The delivery note is made out for the attention of me, Gerd Wolters – so far so good. Now let me check the other details. The quantity, type and item number of the product also match the receiving note. There should be six Meldiva coffee machines in each package, which makes a total of 100 packages. Everything seems fine.

Jan Kowalski: That matches the transportation bill, too. As you can see the goods were dispatched on the 6th of January. The invoice number is 5122 and your order number is 233. And if you'd like to contact your supplier, you can send an email to Jill Cameron. Her email address is: j-i-double l-c-a-m-e-r-o-n-at-s-u-p-e-r-m-a-i-l-dot-co-dot-uk.

Gerd Wolters: Fine. I'll do the first visual check of the goods on the truck. Can you open the back, please?

Jan Kowalski: Yes, sure.

Gerd Wolters: The goods we ordered are given on the label of each package. But there only seem to be 99 packages and one of them is damaged.

Jan Kowalski: Could you write this information on the delivery note and the transportation bill, and then sign both documents, please? Then, I'll countersign them and have two new packages with coffee machines delivered to you immediately.

Gerd Wolters: OK, here's my signature on both documents.

Jan Kowalski: Thanks. And here are copies of the delivery note and the transportation bill for your records.

Gerd Wolters: Fine. Now let's unload the other 98 packages. We can put them on that conveyor belt. Then we'll scan them and give them a secondary check before we store them.

Jan Kowalski: OK, let's start.

A 1.1 Module A Meeting people, A 1, 2

Dialogue 1

Mr Neureuther: Neureuther, good morning.

Ms Hornbach: Good morning, Mr Neureuther.

Mr Neureuther: Good morning, Ms Hornbach.

Ms Hornbach: Mr Neureuther, the young man you were expecting from Denmark is here.

Mr Neureuther: Ah yes, please send him in. And Ms Hornbach, give Mr Dachs a call, will you please?

Ms Hornbach: I've already called him.

Christian: Hello, my name is Christian Eriksen. I come from Fanö in Denmark, and, uh, I'd like to work here as an intern for the next three months.

Mr Neureuther: Felix Neureuther. I'm the manager of the company.

Christian: Nice to meet you, Mr Neureuther.

Mr Neureuther: Nice to meet you too, Christian. I hope you had a pleasant trip.

Christian: Yes, it was fine, thank you. It's not far from Fanö to Kiel.

Mr Neureuther: Fine. Now, let me see, I guess you've handed all the necessary papers over to my secretary, Ms Hornbach?

Christian: Yes, I have.

Mr Neureuther: Oh good, Mr Dachs. I don't believe you've met Christian Eriksen. He'll be our new intern for the next three months. Christian, this is Mr Dachs, our personnel manager.

Mr Dachs: Nice to meet you Christian.

Christian: Nice to meet you too, Mr Dachs.

Mr Neureuther: Christian, Mr Dachs will take you to your team, so you can get to know them all. See you later, Christian.

Christian: See you later, Mr Neureuther.

Dialogue 2:

Mr Dachs: Morning, everybody.

All of them: Good morning, Mr Dachs.

Mr Dachs: I'd like you to meet our new colleague. He'll be working with us for the next three months. He's in his second year of training. Christian, would you like to introduce yourself?

Christian: Hello, my name is Christian Eriksen. I come from Fanö, that's an island off the coast of Denmark. The company I work for is a bit smaller than yours; there's just the boss, a skilled worker and two trainees.

Silke: Hi Christian, nice to meet you. My name is Silke, and I'm also in my second year of training.

Christian: Nice to meet you too, Silke. I'm glad you speak English, because my German is not so fluent. But I'm doing my best to improve.

Silke: No problem, we'll manage.

Josef: Hello Christian, I'm Josef, but everybody calls me Joe. I'm your foreman. My English is not perfect, but Silke can always help. I've been here for quite a long time. Isn't that right, Mr Dachs?

Mr Dachs: Yes, Joe has been with us for over 20 years now. I think for the first few weeks you'll work with him. Well, let's get back to work now. If you have any questions, you can ask Joe, but you can always come to my office, too.

Christian: Thank you, Mr Dachs.

◎ A 3.17 Module 2 Storing and handling goods, A 3, 4

Mr Walker: Hello, Frank.

Frank Löwe: Good morning, Mr Walker.

Mr Walker: Today, I'd like to show you the storage facilities in our logistics centre. We store all kinds of car parts that are delivered later to car factories and car shops. As you can see we store tyres in shelving racks to avoid any kind of damage to them. The tyres aren't individually wrapped and can be easily picked from the rack. Tyres are a good example of non-palletized goods.

Frank Löwe: I see. I'm doing my training in a warehouse that stores food products. The food products usually come in boxes. They're normally stored on pallet racks because the boxes are the same size. The products you have are all different sizes, so you'll need different storage facilities.

Mr Walker: That's right, although the warehouse management system will be the same. We too have to locate products quickly and easily. And we must prevent goods being misplaced or damaged. OK, before we go on, here's a quiz question for you, Frank: How do you store steering wheels?

Frank Löwe: Well, steering wheels are all the same size and they aren't so bulky. Maybe they're stored on pallet racks. A forklift can just place the pallets of steering wheels onto the pallet racks.

Mr Walker: That's right. What about small accessories such as windscreen wipers?

Frank Löwe: Hmh, they are are more difficult to store. Are they placed in bins or baskets?

Mr Walker: Exactly. You know your stuff, Frank. Tomorrow we can look at the warehouse management system in operation. Let's look at some other storage facilties now.

◎ A 1.2 Module B Your company, A 4

Herr Kirchner: OK, so we've covered human resources, accounting, sales and marketing, and purchasing. Now we come to the more technical side of the company, and – of course – the area where you will be spending your time. OK, do you have any questions before we continue?

Sean: Yes, just a general question really. How old is the company?

Herr Kirchner: Older than you, Sean, that's for sure! Krone Elektronik was founded by Dr Florian Krone in 1954, and is still a family-owned company to this day.

Sean: And is this the headquarters here in Bochum?

Herr Kirchner: Yes, it is. Krone has nine manufacturing plants and sales offices across Europe, but this is the largest. In fact, we also have two in the USA – in Chicago and Baltimore.

Sean: Are there any plants in Great Britain?

Herr Kirchner: No, there aren't. But we are opening a new factory in South Korea next year.

Sean: And how many people work for Krone Elektronik?

Herr Kirchner: That's a good question, Sean. I don't know the exact number, but it is at least 10,000, if you include the USA. OK, let's go on with the tour, shall we? The building to your right is our research and development department. They are currently working on a new braking system for a major German car company.

Sean: And what goes on in the large building next to it?

Herr Kirchner: This is our main building, which has three functions. Firstly, it is where the production planners work – and this is where you will spend most of your time. Their job is to optimize the manufacturing process by keeping production times and costs down. Secondly, as you can see, here are also the production halls, where you will start your internship.

Sean: You mentioned three functions. So what else happens over there? It's a really big place.

Herr Kirchner: Yes, it's over 6,000 square metres. Those people you can see over there are responsible for quality control. They test all of the components and devices before they go to the customer.

Sean: How many components are made here in Bochum?

Herr Kirchner: Well, one of the main components we produce here are the cylinder heads, and we make thousands of them every year. And each and every one of them must be inspected by the guys in quality control.

Sean: I guess that's an important job. I'm really looking forward to getting to work.

Herr Kirchner: That's great. I will introduce you to the foreman this afternoon. OK, finally, behind this building we have the IT department. At the moment, they are very busy dealing with the problems caused by our new operating system.

Sean: Oh, that doesn't sound too good. What exactly is the problem?

Herr Kirchner: I'm not sure exactly, some kind of interface difficulties, I think. OK, let's go into the canteen and have some lunch, shall we? Then I can answer some more of your questions.

⊙ A 3.18 Module 3 Moving goods in the warehouse, A 2, 3

Mrs Schneider: Good morning, Mrs Langston, good morning Mr Khan.

Mrs Langston: Good morning, Mrs Schneider.

Mr Khan: Good morning. Thank you for agreeing to give us a guided tour. We hope to see ways of improving our warehouse in Liverpool.

Mrs Schneider: Well, we've done a lot in the last few years to make our handling systems more efficient and, of course, to save time and money. If you'll follow me ... Here on the left you can see the fully automatic handling system which we installed last year.

Mrs Langston: But it must have been very expensive. Is this a future trend now?

Mrs Schneider: Well, there is a trend towards installing more and more automatic systems but it depends on the goods you want to store. In a chemical warehouse, for example, it isn't the first choice. Hazardous goods have to be handled very carefully.

Mr Khan: I see. But why is the automatic system a good choice for your warehouse?

Mrs Schneider: Well, as you know we handle books and paper. They're the same size and have a solid, even surface. Then an automatic system is the best choice.

Mrs Langston: What kind of system are we looking at exactly?

Mrs Schneider: This one is an automatic wheel conveyor. It's often used at the front of the warehouse. It loads and unloads the trucks. This one is robust and has low operating costs.

Mr Khan: I recently read about overhead conveyor systems. When are they used?

Mrs Schneider: Oh yes, they're used in fashion warehouses to transport goods between production areas. We don't have any here.

Mrs Langston: But permanently installed systems have got disadvantages too, don't they?

Mrs Schneider: Yes, that's right. When the systems are permanently installed, they are inflexible. They're also only economical and save money when they run at full capacity. Luckily the systems in our warehouse are always busy. And finally they're expensive and can break down. When that happens, you can't move anything. That's why we don't want to completely give up useful alternatives.

Mrs Langston: What are they then?

Mrs Schneider: Well. We still use lifting carts and forklifts to move pallets of books from one pallet rack to another. They're suitable for any kind of ground transport as they're flexible to use and manoeuver.

Mr Khan: Well, Mrs Schneider. That was really helpful. Thank you very much for the tour.

Mrs Schneider: You're welcome.

⊚ A 1.3 Module C Telephoning, B 5, 6

Alex: Fertighaus Henke, Alex Bauder.

Caller: Yes, hello. Do you speak English?

Alex: Er, yes, a little. How can I help you?

Caller: Well, my name is Matthew Reid and your company is currently building my house. I'm a little confused. I thought this was Mr Deschler's telephone number. He is the construction manager, isn't he?

Alex: Yes, he is, but unfortunately he is off sick today, so all of his calls are being diverted to me. Can I help you with something?

Caller: Well, I was calling to give Mr Deschler some changes to our house.

Alex: OK, and what was your name again, please?

Caller: Reid, Matthew Reid.

Alex: Could you possibly spell that please?

Caller: Certainly. It's R-E-I-D.

Alex: R-I-E-D.

Caller: No, R-E for England, I for India D.

Alex: Sorry, R-E-I-D. OK, Mr Reid, and what is the address of the house?

Caller: Well, so far it is only a foundation pit, but it is Ringstraße 26 in Lernsdorf.

Alex: Ringstraße 26, Lernsdorf. Ah, yes, I know the site. We are scheduled to begin on your cellar next week, I think. OK, if you give me the information, I will pass it on to Mr Deschler. Let me just find a piece of paper … OK, I'm ready.

Caller: First of all, in the kitchen we need to move the extractor fan twenty centimetres to the left, so that it is directly over the hob. And the hole needs to have a diameter of one hundred and eighty-four millimetres, and we also need …

Alex: Sorry Mr Reid, but I am afraid any changes to your kitchen need to be discussed with the kitchen fitters. Are there any changes to the plans for any other part of the house?

Caller: Er, just a moment. Let me look at my list … OK, we need to change the height of the toilets in the bathroom. At the moment they are planned to be forty-five centimetres and we would like them to be fifty. Plus, we need to add another two hundred and twenty volt socket to the right of the bathroom mirror for my electric razor.

Alex: OK, anything else?

Caller: Yes, my wife and I have decided that we will need a larger carport. I have spoken to a friend and he says we should make it eight metres by six metres by three metres. Can you find out how much extra this would cost, please?

Alex: Of course. Let me just confirm, eight metres long by six metres wide. And how high should it be?

Caller: Three metres high. Of course, this means that we will have a smaller garden, but I think a carport is very useful. You can also ask Mr Deschler how big our garden will be with the new carport. It is currently one hundred and thirty-five square metres.

Alex: OK, I will ask him to adjust the plan and get in touch with you as soon as he is back in the office.

Caller: That's great. Oh, just one more thing. My wife wants to put larger windows in the living room. At the moment, the windows in the plan are one hundred and forty-eight centimetres by one hundred and eleven. She would like them to be one hundred and eighty-six by two hundred and twenty-two.

Alex: One eight six by two two two. OK Mr Reid, I will pass this information on to Mr Deschler and ask him to give you a call. Does he have your telephone number?

Caller: Yes, I think so, but let me give you my work number, too. It is 0391 587660… . Thank you for your help Mr Bauder. Goodbye.

Alex: You're welcome Mr Reid. Goodbye.

⊚ A 3.19 Module 4 Picking and consigning goods, A 1

Frank Brown: Hello, Susan. Welcome to our company's warehouse. As you can see here, we use a picking system called 'part-to-picker'. We don't use the picker-to-part system here.

Susan Kelly: Why do you use the part-to-picker system and not the picker-to-part system, Frank?

Frank Brown: Well, that's easy to answer. This is a very big warehouse and it would take too much time to pick the goods by hand. As you probably know, in the picker-to-part system the order pickers get a picking list and take the goods from the shelves; or sometimes they receive their orders electronically by headsets.

Susan Kelly: OK, but what do you need to operate your part-to-picker system?

Frank Brown: You need three things. Firstly a storage area for the goods. Secondly, a picking area where the automatic part-to-picker system takes the goods from their storage places. And thirdly, a material handling system which transports the goods to the picking bays.

Susan Kelly: I see. And what happens at the picking bays then?

Frank Brown: When the goods arrive at the different picking bays, the picking operator at each picking bay receives exactly the items he or she needs for an order and prepares them for dispatch.

Susan Kelly: OK, and then the order picking process is completed and the goods can be packed and consigned.

Frank Brown: Yes, that's right.

Susan Kelly: Thank you very much for explaining this to me, Frank. That was very interesting.

Frank Brown: You're very welcome, Susan.

A 3.20 Module 5 Packing goods, A 2

Florian Steinbach: Hello, Mr Miles.

Sean Miles: Hi! Please call me Sean.

Florian Steinbach: OK! I'm Florian. I'd really like to find out more about the packaging you use here for all the different products.

Sean Miles: OK, Florian. I'll be very happy to explain that to you. As you know, nowadays many products are transported over long distances.

Florian Steinbach: Yes, so the packaging must protect the goods against humidity, extreme temperatures and perhaps even insects. Right?

Sean Miles: Exactly. And there are lots of different forms of packaging.

Florian Steinbach: Yes, I know, for example, crates, barrels, bales, containers, sacks, pallets and so on.

Sean Miles: That's right. And different products need different packing. Think of fragile products made of glass, for example. They might get dropped and broken during transport. So they need to be protected against that.

Florian Steinbach: Yeah, and that's why we put handling symbols on the packaging, too. That way everybody knows how to handle the goods.

Sean Miles: Right and adequate packaging also means that goods can be stacked more easily and that more goods can be transported at the same time.

Florian Steinbach: What about the storage of the goods?

Sean Miles: That's another important point, Florian. Good packaging means that you don't waste space in pallet racks, for example. It also shows the bar code you need so that the computer system can reorder the product, if necessary.

Florian Steinbach: I see. Thanks a lot, Sean.

Sean Miles: You're very welcome, Florian. See you.

Florian Steinbach: Goodbye.

A 1.4 Module E Applications, C 1

Andrea: Hi David, how are you doing?

David: Hi Andrea. I'm fine thanks. How are you?

Andrea: Yeah, I'm OK. Busy, but fine.

David: I heard that you were thinking about applying for a three-month internship in the Northampton branch. Is that true?

Andrea: Yes, that's right. I really want to spend some time in England. I guess it was the same with you and coming to Germany.

David: Exactly. I wanted to see how things worked over here. So, you want to spend some time with my old colleagues, eh? That's great.

Andrea: Well actually, I wanted to ask you for a bit of advice if that's OK with you?

David: Sure, what can I help you with?

Andrea: Well, I have to officially apply for the internship, which means a letter and a CV.

David: OK, would you like me to read your letter?

Andrea: Yes, that would be great. I am going to finish it this weekend, and then I will bring it to work on Monday. Thanks. But where I really need your advice is with the CV. I was wondering if you had any tips for me. I know there are some differences between German and English CVs.

David: Yes, there are, you're right. Hmm ... tips ... let me see. OK, the first thing to remember is that your CV should be no longer than two pages.

Andrea: Two pages, OK.

David: Also, make sure you use good-quality paper and never send your CV without a covering letter.

Andrea: OK ...

David: And don't forget to highlight your strengths and achievements. And when you talk about your work experience, start with your most recent job.

Andrea: Do I need to include a picture?

David: In England, a CV does not have a picture, but you can have one if you like. What is important is that you include the name and contact details of two references. These could be a supervisor or maybe a teacher.

Andrea: OK, great. Anything else?

David: Yeah, make sure that everything you write in your CV is the truth. If you are asked to explain something during the interview and you can't, then it could be pretty embarrassing. Be confident and sell yourself, but don't lie. Er ... once you have finished the CV, read through it and check the spelling and the grammar. The best thing to do is to give it to a friend. And, when you send it, keep a copy for yourself to read before the interview.

Andrea: Thanks a lot for the advice, David. I'm really grateful.

David: Don't mention it, Andrea. Let me know if there is anything else I can do.

Andrea: Well ... you did say somebody should read over it and check everything – and who'd be better than a native speaker ...?

◎ A 3.21 Module 6 Handling dangerous goods, B 2, 3

Paul Gray: Good morning, Hakan. How are you?

Hakan Bulut: I'm fine, thank you, Paul.

Paul Gray: OK, Hakan. Let's get started. Today, we've got lots of dangerous goods to pack and load. I can see you've already put the cardboard boxes in the right place here.

Hakan Bulut: Yes, I have. And I've already put the barrels with liquid chemicals and the safety cans with propane gas here, but we still need to get them ready for loading.

Paul Gray: Good. So here are the UN number labels.

Hakan Bulut: What are they for? I thought it would be enough to put the right warning signs on the packaging.

Paul Gray: No, that's not enough. The UN number labels must also be put on the packaging to label the goods as dangerous. Each label has four different numbers that tell you how dangerous the products are. If an accident happens, then people know exactly what to do.

Hakan Bulut: I see. But there are no numbers on the UN labels yet.

Paul Gray: That's right and that'll be your job now: you prepare the UN labels by reading the numbers on the goods we have to pack and writing them on the UN number labels.

Hakan Bulut: OK, no problem. I'll do that.

Paul Gray: First, we've got some corrosive liquids here. They're not as dangerous as many other goods, so we can just use two cardboard boxes with dividers to separate them from each other. Have you already prepared the UN number labels?

Hakan Bulut: Yes, here you are.

Paul Gray: Thanks. Let's put the goods in the boxes, close them with adhesive tape and put the UN number labels on them. Is there anything else we need to do?

Hakan Bulut: Yes, we need to put the right warning sign on the boxes.

Paul Gray: Correct, Hakan. And how is the flammable propane gas bottled?

Hakan Bulut: It's bottled in safety cans to make sure that the gas doesn't come out. And liquid chemicals must be bottled in solid barrels to make sure nothing leaks out.

Paul Gray: Fine. Now put the UN number labels on the cardboard box, the safety cans and the barrels. And please don't forget the warning signs. I've got to do some other work now but I'll be back later to check everything once more.

Hakan Bulut: OK, see you later then.

◎ A 1.5 Module F Socialising, A 1

Fabian: Hi, I'm Fabian.

Jan: Hello Fabian, my name's Jan. I'm with the group from Warsaw, Poland.

Fabian: Welcome to our company. Is this your first visit to Germany?

Jan: Actually, I've been here before. But my German isn't very good.

Fabian: Don't worry, we can talk in English. I should really practice more anyway. How was your trip? Was it a long journey?

Jan: No, not really. We took the plane from Warsaw to Stuttgart. Then someone from your company met us at the airport.

Fabian: Jan, would you like something to drink: coffee, juice, lemonade?

Jan: Sure, a lemonade would be good.

Fabian: OK, let's go to our canteen and sit down for a while.

Fabian: Here we go; I hope it's cold enough.

Jan: Thanks. So, I guess that you are also a trainee. What year are you in?

Fabian: I'm in my third year. What about you?
Jan: I've just started. How many trainees are there in your company?
Fabian: Er … about ten, I think.
Jan: That's quite a lot. There are only three trainees in our company, all in metal engineering. I think your company is much bigger than ours.
Fabian: Yeah, we even have our own football team. We don't play in a league; it's just for fun.
Jan: That sounds great! You should visit us in Poland one day. Maybe we could arrange a match.
Fabian: That's a good idea. Are you a football fan?
Jan: Yeah. I don't play myself, but I like to watch.
Fabian: Which team do you like?
Jan: Manchester United.
Fabian: Really? They're my favourite team, too! Well, apart from VFB Stuttgart, of course.
Jan: Do you live in Stuttgart?
Fabian: No, I live in a small town nearby. I have to take the bus every morning. But when the weather's good, I can take my motorbike.
Jan: Cool! Unfortunately I don't have a motorbike. I get a lift from a colleague who works in the same department as me.
Fabian: What do you do in your free time?
Jan: I like going to clubs, and sometimes I go fishing with my friends. What about you? Playing football, I suppose.
Fabian: Yeah, football and riding my motorbike.

⦾ A 3.22 Module 7 Shipping goods, B 2

Luke: Hello, Tom.
Tom: Hi, Luke. Alright? I've been thinking about the conversation we had yesterday. You asked me to explain how the transportation of goods can be organised best.
Luke: Yes, that's right, Tom.
Tom: Well, I have some time now, so let me explain it to you. As you know, we have lots of customers overseas.
Luke: Yeah, I know. We deliver goods to India, Australia, Brazil, the USA and other countries all over the world.
Tom: That's right. And tomorrow we're going to send 300 tons of glass products to Brazil. Now, what's the first thing we should think about when packing these goods, Luke? What do you think?
Luke: Well, they're glass products which means they could break very easily. So first of all they must be packed carefully. Then the consignment must be labeled as fragile to make sure that it's handled correctly and arrives safely at the customer's warehouse.
Tom: That's right. But there're more things to think about before the goods can leave our warehouse. Any ideas?
Luke: Well, mmh … I guess it's not just our decision which means of transport we use, is it?
Tom: OK. Why not?
Luke: Maybe the customer needs the products very urgently. Then we have to look at the schedule and decide when the consignment must leave our warehouse at the latest and how it should be transported to the buyer.
Tom: And we must always think about the costs when choosing a means of transport, too.
Luke: Yes, that's why it's important to talk about this with the customer first, so that we know how much he is willing to pay.
Tom: Exactly. We have to discuss various means of transport or even alternative transport routes. OK, I hope that's clear now. I've got to go, Luke.
Luke: Thanks a lot, Tom.
Tom: You're welcome. See you later then.
Luke: Yeah, goodbye.

⦾ A 1.6 Module G Presentations, C 1

Good morning ladies and gentlemen. Today I would like to present our new range of wooden furniture, Simply Wood. The range, which is shown here on the first slide, includes chairs, a large table, a lounger, and benches. I would like to start by talking about the materials used in the furniture. All of the Simply Wood range is made from single softwood timber and has been hand-crafted by our highly-skilled carpenters and joiners. If you look at this picture, you can see that the benches and the seats are designed with a low back, deep seats and long arms to offer a great deal of comfort and convenience. Thanks to a special varnish, the furniture is 100% weatherproof and will not suffer from discolouring. As you can see from this final slide, the furniture is also available in white, to give it a classic, timeless look. And do not worry, we have used a durable, white polyurethane coating that is suitable for every environment. On your handout you will see more details about each piece, including measurements. Thank you for your attention this morning. Are there any questions? Yes …

⊙ A 3.23 Module 8 Waste disposal and the environment, A 2

Richard Green: Good morning, Mrs Hughes and welcome to our school. It's really nice to have you here today. We've invited you to talk about waste management. This is a very important worldwide issue and we really appreciate your coming to tell us more about it. The students have prepared some questions that they would like to ask you.

Samantha Hughes: Thank you very much for inviting me, Mr Green. I'm very happy to answer any questions the students might have. So, what would you like to know?

Carlos: Hello, Mrs Hughes. I have a question, please. Are there any principles on how companies should deal with waste?

Samantha Hughes: Yes, there are. First of all they should try to avoid producing waste as much as possible. I think that's a very important principle to start with.

Carlos: I agree with you, but it's easier said than done.

Samantha Hughes: That's true. But it's a necessary first step. It can be achieved by using more efficient machines, improving packaging and choosing the right means of transport. These are just a few examples of how we can try to reduce our environmental impact.

Susan: But what other steps are there?

Samantha Hughes: Another really important step is to recycle waste and put it back into the economic cycle. There are some examples of this in our private lives, too. For example, what do you do with empty deposit bottles?

David: We collect them at home and then return them to the supermarket where we bought them.

Samantha Hughes: That's right and this way the bottles are put back into the economic cycle.

Andy: But I don't think all waste can be recycled. Right?

Samantha Hughes: Yes, that's correct and it's a big problem. Some waste has to be disposed of because it can't be recycled. Sometimes recycling just doesn't make sense and it's more environmentally friendly to dispose of the waste.

Richard Green: Thank you very much, Mrs Hughes. I think we'll have a short break now and continue our discussion later on.

⊙ A 1.7 Module H Dealing with customers, A 4

Answering machine: Guten Tag. Sie sind mit Stefan Bauder verbunden. Leider bin ich im Moment nicht erreichbar. Bitte hinterlassen Sie eine Nachricht nach dem Ton. Danke!

Brian: Hello Mr Bauder, this is Brian Jenkins calling from New Wave Marketing in Hamburg. I am calling about the new IT network that your technicians set up last week. Unfortunately, we have been experiencing some problems. Since your technicians were here, some employees have had difficulty connecting to the Internet, and others have no access to our network at all and cannot even log on to their computers! However, the worst thing is that some important files and documents seem to have been lost as a result of the migration to the new software. One of these files was a presentation for a very important client. This is a particular problem for us because we have a meeting with this client on Monday, and we need the presentation and do not have enough time to redo it. Could you please look into this problem for us urgently as time is running out? If we do not hear from you by the end of today, we will have to look elsewhere. I will be in meetings this afternoon, but you can contact me per email under B dot Jenkins at NWM…de. Thank you.

Grammar overview

Present Tense (Gegenwart)

Bildung: Present Tense (simple)		
Merke: Bei der 3. Person Einzahl *(he / she / it)* wird ein *s* an die Endung des Verbs angehängt.	I like / you like / he (she / it) likes we like / you like / they like	computer games.

Verwendung: Present Tense (simple)	
– bei allgemein bekannten Tatsachen und Aussagen	– Most cars run on petrol.
– bei regelmäßigen Handlungen: Schlüsselwörter: *usually, normally, always, never, sometimes, often …*	– I usually start work at 7 o'clock.
– bei Gewohnheiten	– He doesn't smoke.
– bei Fahrplänen, Öffnungszeiten etc. für die Zukunft	– My train leaves at 10 o'clock tomorrow morning.

Bildung: Present Tense (progressive)		
am / are / is + Infinitiv mit Endung *-ing*	I **am** / you **are** / he / she / it / **is** we **are** / you **are** / they **are**	work**ing** on a new project.

Verwendung: Present Tense (progressive)	
– bei Handlungen im Augenblick des Sprechens	– I am reading a manual at the moment.
– bei vorübergehenden Handlungen	– I'm staying at the Royal Excelsior Hotel.
– bei (fest) geplanten Handlungen in der Zukunft	– I'm meeting Ms Winter next week.
– bei gefühlsbetonten Aussagen mit *always* (negativ besetzt)	– He is always complaining about his boss.

Past Tense (Vergangenheit)

Bildung: Past Simple	
ed-Endung bei regelmäßigen Verben	I work**ed** in Munich last year.
2. Form bei unregelmäßigen Verben *(1. meet / **2. met** / 3. met)*	He **met** Mr Miller yesterday.

Verwendung: Past Simple		
Bei Vorgängen, die in der Vergangenheit abgeschlossen wurden; oft mit Zeitangabe. Signalwörter u. a.: *yesterday, in (1990), two weeks ago, last year, last month, last week.*	I finished my studies	in 2008. 3 years ago. last week.

Present Perfect (Vollendete Gegenwart)

Bildung: Present Perfect (simple)		
have oder *has* + *ed*-Endung (bei regelmäßigen Verben)	I / you / we / they **have** work**ed** He / she **has** work**ed**	as a trainee.
	It **has** work**ed** well for us.	
3. Form bei unregelmäßigen Verben *(1. see / 2. saw / **3. seen**)*	I have **seen** the new car.	

Bildung: Present Perfect (progressive)		
have / has + *been* + Infinitiv mit *-ing*	I / you / we / they **have** He / she **has**	**been** liv**ing** in Munich for 5 years.

Verwendung: Present Perfect (simple and progressive)	
– bei Handlungen in der Vergangenheit **ohne Zeitangabe**	– I have written three letters.
– bei noch andauernden Zeitbestimmungen	– We haven't had any complaints so far / today …
– bei Handlungen, die in der Vergangenheit begonnen haben, aber noch nicht abgeschlossen sind, wobei ***for*** bei Zeiträumen *(two hours / three weeks)* und ***since*** bei Zeitpunkten *(2001 / January)* benutzt wird	– I have been living in Stuttgart **for** 20 years. – I have been living in Stuttgart **since** 1982.
– Einige Verben werden in der Regel nicht in der Verlaufsform verwendet.	– I have **had** the car for five years. – I have **known** the company since 2010.

Future (Zukunft)

Bildung und Verwendung	
Shall / will drückt äußere Umstände aus.	Most of this year's teleworking jobs **will** be offered in autumn.
Will drückt die Bereitschaft oder Entschlossenheit aus, etwas zu tun, sowie Versprechungen. ***Will*** wird auch benutzt für eine spontane Entscheidung.	I'**ll** do my best to get the job. Wait a minute, I'**ll** help you!
Going to wird verwendet, um persönliche Planungen und Vorhaben auszudrücken. ***Going to*** wird auch verwendet, wenn bereits Anzeichen dafür da sind, dass etwas eintreten wird.	I **am going to** apply for a job in teleworking. *(Ich habe vor…)* Look at those clouds! It'**s going to** rain.
Present continuous wird verwendet, um eine feste Vereinbarung (gewöhnlich mit Zeitangabe) mitzuteilen.	Jennifer is **meeting** her colleague this evening.
Present simple wird für die Zukuft verwendet in Verbindung mit Fahrplänen, Öffnungszeiten usw.	Jim's train **arrives** at 4.30 p.m. Our office **opens** at 9 o'clock tomorrow morning.

Comparison of adjectives (Steigerung des Adjektivs)

Bildung	
Einsilbige und zweisilbige Adjektive werden durch Anhängen von *-er* und *-est* (germanische Steigerung) gesteigert. Aus ***y*** wird ***i***. Ein einzelner Endkonsonant wird nach einfachem betonten Vokal verdoppelt.	fast – faster – fastest easy – easier – easiest hot – hotter – hottest
Für die zweisilbigen gibt es keine eindeutigen Regeln. Gewöhnlich werden zweisilbige Adjektive, die auf *-y*, *-le*, *-er* oder *-ow* enden germanisch gesteigert, aber dies ist keine bindende Regel.	clever – cleverer – cleverest noble – nobler – noblest narrow – narrower – narrowest
Ebenfalls germanisch gesteigert werden zweisilbige Adjektive, wenn sie ihre Betonung auf der zweiten Silbe haben. Auch diese Regel ist nicht bindend. Daneben gibt es aber z. B. auch folgende Formen: *more / the most clever* oder *more / the most polite.*	polite – politer – politest sincere – sincerer – sincerest
Andere zweisilbige Adjektive werden in der Regel romanisch gesteigert.	nervous – more nervous – most nervous splendid – more splendid – most splendid
Alle drei- und mehrsilbigen Adjektive steigert man mit ***more*** und ***the most*** (romanische Steigerung).	expensive – more expensive – the most expensive beautiful – more beautiful – the most beautiful
Es gibt auch eine Reihe von unregelmäßigen Adjektiven.	good – better – the best bad – worse – the worst much / many – more – the most little – less – the least old – elder – the eldest (bei Familienangehörigen)

Verwendung	
Gleichheiten mit *as … as*	He is **as** skilful **as** I. (so geschickt / fachmännisch wie ich)
Komparative mit *than*	Mike is **less** helpful **than** Tim. (weniger … als)
Je … desto…	**The** more I work with this machine **the** better I like it.
Superlativ beim Vergleich von mehr als zwei Objekten	The new electric drill is **the most** expensive tool in the brochure.

Adverbs (Adverbien)

Das Umstandswort (Adverb) dient zur näheren Beschreibung eines Eigenschaftswortes (Adjektives) oder eines Zeitwortes (Verbs).

Bildung	
Von der Wortbildung her unterscheidet man zwei Arten von Adverbien:	
1. ursprüngliche und durch Zusammensetzung gebildete Adverbien	often, quite, here, soon always, already, yesterday
2. durch Ableitung gebildete Abverbien: Hier wird an das Adjektiv ein *-ly* angehängt.	clear**ly**, usual**ly**, quick**ly**, easi**ly**, bad**ly**
Manche Adjektive und Adverbien sind	
- gleichlautend oder	daily, weekly, monthly, yearly, early, fast
- unterschiedlich.	good – **well**
Die Steigerung des Adverbs ist der Steigerung des Adjektivs vergleichbar.	carefully – more carefully – most carefully fast – faster – the fastest
Unregelmäßige Formen der Steigerung	well – better – best badly – worse – worst
y wird zu ***i***	happy + -ly = happily
stummes *e* fällt weg	true + -ly = truly
Verdoppelung des Endkonsonanten	beautiful + -ly = beautifully

Verwendung	
Hier wird das Verb näher beschrieben.	The new machine **works well.**
Hier wird das Adjektiv *clear* näher beschrieben.	The small printer makes **remarkably clear** printouts.
Hier wird ein anderes Adverb *(quickly)* näher beschrieben.	Our new machine works **extremely quickly**.

Questions (Fragen)

Bildung: Alternative questions (Entscheidungsfragen)	
Entscheidungsfragen, die mit ja oder nein beantwortet werden können, werden im Englischen immer mit einem Hilfsverb oder einer Form von *to do* eingeleitet.	**Do** you smoke? **Did** you see Mr Miller yesterday?
Erstes Hilfsverb steht vor dem Subjekt.	**Have** you met Mr Miller?

Verwendung: Alternative questions (Entscheidungsfragen)	
Does Sally speak French?	Yes, she **does.** / No, she **doesn't.**
Can these tools be used in milling as well as in turning?	Yes, they **can.** / No, they **can't.**
Is the lathe set properly for this job?	Yes, it **is.** / No, it **isn't.**
Did he meet the chief executive at the fair?	Yes, he **did.** / No, he **didn't.**
Will you finish this job by Friday?	Yes, I **will.** / No, I **won't.**

Bildung: Questions with interrogatives (Fragen mit Fragefürwörtern)	
Die Fragen werden mit dem Fragefürwort eingeleitet. Vor dem Subjekt steht die Form von *to do (do / does; did)*, nach dem Subjekt steht das Vollverb im Infinitiv.	**How** do you **go** to work? **What** does she **do**?
Wird nach dem Subjekt oder einem Teil des Subjekts gefragt *(who, what, which, whose)*, so wird die Form von 'to do' nicht verwendet.	**What** is his job?

Verwendung: Questions with interrogatives (Fragen mit Fragefürwörtern)	
Fragewort ist Subjekt.	Who operates this machine? Which tools do you need for this job?
Fragewort ist nicht Subjekt.	Who / Whom did he meet at the exhibition? Which tool have you chosen for this job?

Word order (Wortstellung)

Bildung	
Die Wortstellung folgt im englischen Aussagesatz der Regel S – P – O: *Subject [They] – Predicate [have repaired] – Object [the broken tools]*	They have repaired the broken tools.
Dies gilt auch im Nebensatz (im Deutschen steht ja im Nebensatz das Prädikat am Ende).	I was told that they had repaired the broken tools.
Zeitbestimmungen stehen in der Regel entweder am Anfang oder am Ende des Satzes.	Yesterday they repaired the broken tools. They repaired the broken tools a week ago.
Mehrere Umstandsbestimmungen folgen gewöhnlich folgender Reihenfolge: *Manner – Place – Time* (Art und Weise – Ort – Zeit)	The mechanic repaired the tools in the shop yesterday. The mechanic repaired the tools quite skilfully in the shop last night.
Adverbien der Häufigkeit *(frequency)* können auch vor dem Hauptverb stehen: *always, ever, never, often, regularly, generally, rarely, seldom, occasionally.* Diese Adverbien stehen aber nach dem Verb *to be.* Bei Hilfsverben stehen die Adverbien der Häufigkeit zwischen dem Hilfsverb und dem Vollverb, bzw. nach dem Hilfsverb.	The service people **always** come on time. The service people **never** come without calling ahead. The service people **usually** check the machine in May. They are **generally** very reliable. The machine has **sometimes** had problems. With old machines you can **never** tell.

Defining relative clauses (Notwendige Relativsätze)

Ein Relativsatz ist notwendig, wenn die darin gegebene Information nötig ist, um deutlich zu machen, welche Person oder Sache gemeint ist.

Verwendung	
bei Personen ***who*** oder ***that***	The man **who / that** is operating the CNC machine usually works at the training centre.
bei Sachen ***which*** oder ***that***	The machine element **which / that** is moving the tool is the main spindle.
im Genitiv wird **whose** verwendet	Tom is an engineer **whose** skills are highly praised.
Das Relativpronomen als Satzobjekt kann weggelassen werden.	They called the technician (**who**) they saw standing at the milling machine. Sally read the operation plan (**which**) she had filled in this morning.

Non-defining relative clauses (Nicht notwendige Relativsätze)

Ein Relativsatz ist nicht notwendig, wenn die darin gegebene Information nicht nötig ist, um deutlich zu machen, welche Person oder Sache gemeint ist.

Verwendung	
Ein Relativsatz ist nicht notwendig, wenn die darin enthaltene Information nicht nötig ist, um zu erkennen, welche Person oder Sache gemeint ist.	**Sally's friend**, who is a skilled worker, **is doing his final exams this summer**. **The machine**, which is DEG's latest model, **works perfectly**.
Relativpronomen als Satzobjekt	**The three German apprentices**, who Sally met at the training centre, **are in their last year of training.**

Reported speech (Indirekte Rede)

Die indirekte Rede wird benutzt, wenn berichtet wird oder wurde, was jemand sagt oder sagte, bzw. macht oder machte (**Aussage**), wenn jemandem gesagt wird oder wurde, was geschehen soll (**Aufforderung**), oder wenn gefragt wird oder wurde, was geschieht oder geschah (**Frage**).

Bildung / Verwendung	
Steht das Wort, welches die indirekte Rede einleitet, in der Gegenwart, so ändern sich die Zeitformen der direkten Rede nicht.	"We **are measuring** this machined component." → Sally explains that they are measuring the machined component.
Steht das Wort, welches die indirekte Rede einleitet, in der Vergangenheit, so ändern sich die Zeitformen der direkten Rede wie folgt.	
Simple past und *present perfect* werden zu *past perfect.*	Sally **explained that they were measuring** the machined component. "The trainee **forgot** to set the revolution speed." → The master **noticed that the trainee had forgotten** to check the revolution speed.
Will wird zu *would.*	"The drilling operation **will** have to be prepared by marking out and centring." → Oliver **remembered** that the drilling operation **would** have to be prepared by marking out and centring.
Pronomen werden angepasst.	"**I can't** find the measuring equipment." → **Sally told** me that she **couldn't find** the measuring equipment.
Orts- und Zeitbestimmungen werden angepasst.	"**We** are seeing the other students **tomorrow.**" → Oliver **added** that **they** were seeing the other students **the next day.** "I programmed the CNC machine **two days ago.**" → He said that he had programmed the CNC machine **two days earlier.**
Aufforderungen werden in der indirekten Rede im Infinitiv wiedergegeben.	"**Use** HSS twist drills to drill metal stock." → The instructor **advised** Sally **to use** HSS twist drills to drill metal stock.
Bei Fragen wird die Wortstellung wie im Aussagesatz verwendet, d. h. am Anfang steht das Fragewort, dann folgen Subjekt, Prädikat und Objekt.	"Why has Oliver used the impact drilling function?" → The master **wanted to know why Oliver had used** the impact drilling function. "When did you sharpen the drill?" → He asked **when he had sharpened** the drill.
Die Umschreibung mit 'to do' wird nur bei Verneinungen angewendet.	"Why **don't** you call the salesman?" → She **asked** Sally why she **didn't call** the salesman.

Passive voice (Passiv)

Bildung	
Form von *to be* + *ed*-Endung (wie bei *simple past*) bei regelmäßigen Verben Form von *to be* + 3. Form bei unregelmäßigen Verben (*1. take/2. took/3.* ***taken***. Siehe Liste der unregelmäßigen Verben.)	The machine is equipped with an emergency stop. He **is taken** to hospital.

Aktiv:	We *Subjekt*	recharge *Prädikat*	the batteries. *Objekt*
Passiv:	*Subjekt* The batteries	*Prädikat* are recharged	*Objekt (by-agent)* (by us).

Formen	
Present Tense (Simple)	The goods are transported every day.
Present Tense (Progressive)	The goods are being transported at the moment.
Past Tense (Simple)	The goods were transported yesterday.
Past Tense (Progressive)	The goods were being transported when the truck crashed.
Future 1 (will)	The goods will be transported next Monday, I promise.
Future 1 (going to)	The goods are going to be transported next month.
Present Perfect	The goods have already been transported.
Past Perfect	The goods had been transported before the order arrived.

Verwendung	
Das Passiv wird hauptsächlich verwendet, wenn der Ausführende (*by-agent*) unwichtig oder unbekannt ist oder nicht genannt werden soll. Deshalb wird der *by-agent* nur bei besonderer Betonung genannt.	The batteries **are recharged** (**by us**) when they are empty. A few years ago the first cars **were equipped** with airbags (**by the manufacturers**).
Die Passivkonstruktion wird besonders bei technischen Beschreibungen, Anweisungen in Handbüchern usw. verwendet. Bei der Umwandlung von Aktiv in Passiv wird das Objekt des Aktivsatzes zum Subjekt des Passivsatzes.	Aktiv: We recharge **the batteries.** Passiv: **The batteries** are recharged (by us).
Im Gegensatz zum Deutschen können bestimmte Verben im Englischen im Passiv verwendet werden. Die Übersetzung ins Deutsche erfolgt durch eine Konstruktion mit 'man'.	The fuel cell is considered to be a very promising invention. *(Man hält die Brennstoffzelle für eine sehr zukunftsweisende Erfindung.)*
Die Verlaufsform ist im Passiv nur im *Present Tense* und *Past Tense* gebräuchlich.	He **is being** taken to hospital. *(Er wird gerade ins Krankenhaus gebracht.)* He **was being** taken to hospital. *(Er wurde gerade ins Krankenhaus gebracht.)*

Gerund (Gerundium)

Wie im Deutschen kann man auch im Englischen aus einem Verb ein Substantiv machen. Beispiel: Durch häufiges **Messen** können Fehler vermieden werden.

Bildung		
Anhängen von *-ing* an den Infinitiv (Grundform) des Verbs	check + ing = checking drill + ing = drilling	
Verdoppelung eines Endkonsonanten (Mitlaut) nach einem Vokal (Selbstlaut)	put – putting control – controlling	travel – travelling refuel – refuelling
Stummes *e* fällt weg: aber: *agree – agreeing; see – seeing*	file – filing measure – measuring	

Verwendung	
Ein *gerund* kann Subjekt (Satzgegenstand) sein. Ebenso kann es die Funktion eines Objekts (Satzergänzung) haben.	**Filing** is rarely done by hand. He began **cleaning** the machine.
Nach Präpositionen (Verhältniswörtern) oder präpositionalen Ausdrücken steht ebenfalls das *gerund*.	He was afraid of **setting** the lever to a higher speed. They objected **to trying** the new software **without having** made a backup of the hard drive. The manager apologised **for being** late. They prevented the visitors **from entering** the production area without a hard hat. He was tired **of hearing** the same complaint.
Nach bestimmten Verben (Zeitwörtern) steht das *gerund*.	Try to **avoid overheating** the machine. The trainer **recommended turning** the machine off. We cannot **risk losing** this customer. Phillip **suggested using** a different production method.
Weitere Verben, die ein *gerund* nach sich haben.	enjoy, like, dislike, remember, stop He enjoys working in Italy.

Prepositions (Verhältniswörter)

Präpositionen geben das Verhältnis von Personen oder Dingen zueinander an (z. B. räumlich oder zeitlich).

Räumliche Präpositionen			
above	oberhalb	**into**	in … hinein
across	durch, quer durch	**off**	von … herunter, von … weg
at	neben, bei	**on, upon**	auf
opposite	gegenüber		

Räumliche Präpositionen			
behind	hinter	**out, out of**	aus, heraus
below	unter, unterhalb	**through**	durch
beneath	unter, unterhalb	**to**	zu, nach, in Richtung auf
beside	neben	**towards**	auf … zu (Richtung)
between	zwischen	**under**	unter
in	in	**within**	innerhalb

Zeitliche Präpositionen			
at	an, in	**from**	von
before	vor	**in**	am, im (Jahre)
between	zwischen	**on**	an, am
by	bis, bis spätestens	**since**	seit (Zeitpunkt)
during	während	**until, till**	bis
for	seit (Zeitraum)		

Modale Präpositionen und Präpositionen des Grundes			
according to	entsprechend, gemäß	**despite, in spite of**	trotz
because of	wegen	**with**	mit
besides	außer	**without**	ohne

Verwendung	
Laut Gebrauchsanweisung sollte **das Auswechseln** der Werkzeuge kein Problem darstellen.	**According to** the manual, there should be no problem **with** changing the tools.
… **hinten** im Raum … **unten** auf jeder Seite … **am** Eingang	The machine is **at** the back of the room. You'll find the number of the module **at** the bottom of every page. They were waiting **at** the entrance when it happened.
… ist **gegenüber / auf der anderen Seite** … rannte quer **über** die Straße	The printer is **across** the hall. The dog ran **across** the road.
… **zwischen** zwei Aktenmappen (räumlich) … **zwischen** 9 und 10 Uhr (zeitlich)	He found the letter **between** two folders. Why don't we meet **between** nine and ten?
… nur **während**	Smoking is allowed **during** the lunch break only!
… **von** … **bis**	He worked in Cardiff **from** December **until** January.
… **auf** der Straße	You should not park your car **in** the street.
… **bis** (spätestens)	You must be back **by** six o'clock at the latest.

Modal auxiliaries (Modale Hilfsverben)

Die modalen Hilfsverben werden im Englischen oft auch *defective* (d.h. unvollständige) *auxiliaries* genannt, denn sie können in der Regel nur das Präsens bilden. Für die übrigen Zeiten müssen Ersatzformen verwendet werden.

Bildung

Hilfsverb	**Ersatzform**	**deutsche Bedeutung**
can	to be able to	können, fähig sein, in der Lage sein
can	to be allowed to	dürfen, die Erlaubnis haben
may	to be allowed to	dürfen, die Erlaubnis haben
must	to have to	müssen
mustn't	not to be allowed to	nicht dürfen
needn't	not to have to	nicht brauchen, nicht müssen

Verwendung

Present Tense: You **must** read the installation instructions very carefully. After the installation is completed you **needn't reboot** your system.	**Simple past:** Yesterday he **had to** read the installation instructions twice because they were badly translated. I **didn't have to** reboot my system when I installed the screensaver the other day.
Present Tense: He **can** handle software problems quite well.	**Present perfect:** Up to now he **has been able** to handle software problems quite well.
Present Tense: You **must not smoke** in the office.	**Future:** You **will not be allowed** to smoke in the office.

Participles (Partizipien)

Bildung

Present Participle Infinitiv + *-ing*	Wind turbines are a **promising** option.
Past Participle 3. Stammform: ***damaged*** (*ed*-Endung wie bei *simple past*); (3. Form bei unregelmäßigen Verben: *1. know / 2. knew /* ***3. known***. Siehe Liste der unregelmäßigen Verben.)	After the storm we had to replace three **damaged** solar panels.

Verwendung	
als Adjektiv	It is a **known** fact that solar power can be used as an alternative energy.
Partizipialkonstruktionen dienen zur **Verkürzung** von:	
1. adverbialen Nebensätzen mit Konjunktion *(when, although, as, while,...)*	When **planning** to build a home, you should consider using solar energy to heat your water.
2. adverbialen Nebensätzen ohne Konjunktion	**Unlocking** the warehouse door, he smelled gas.
3. Relativsätzen	Wind farms **built** along the coast are most efficient.
Partizipialkonstruktionen zur **Verknüpfung** von zwei Hauptsätzen.	The guide led us through the factory. He warned us to stay away from the machines. The guide led us through the factory **warning** us to stay away from the machines.

If-clauses (Bedingungssätze)

Man unterscheidet drei Arten von Bedingungen:
1. erfüllbare Bedingungen
2. Bedingungen, deren Erfüllung unwahrscheinlich ist
3. Bedingungen, die überhaupt nicht mehr erfüllt werden können.

Zusätzlich zu den drei Typen gibt es noch einen weiteren Typ, der Regeln und Naturgesetze ausdrückt.

Bildung und Verwendung	
Type I (probable condition)	If you **lubricate** this machine regularly, it **will run** smoothly for a long time. *(Wenn man die Maschine regelmäßig ölt, läuft sie lange Zeit problemlos.)*
Type II (improbable condition)	If you **lubricated** this machine regularly, **it would** run smoothly for a long time. *(Wenn man diese Maschine regelmäßig ölen würde, würde sie für lange Zeit problemlos laufen.)*
Type III (impossible condition)	If you **had lubricated** this machine regularly, it **would have run** smoothly for a long time. *(Wenn man die Maschine regelmäßig geölt hätte, wäre sie lange Zeit problemlos gelaufen (jetzt läuft sie aber offensichtlich nicht mehr).*
Rules and laws of nature Hier handelt es sich im eigentlichen Sinne nicht mehr um eine Bedingung, sondern um ein Naturgesetz. Deshalb steht im Hauptsatz auch kein Futur, sondern ebenfalls das Präsens.	If you **heat** ice, it **melts**. *(Wenn man Eis erhitzt, schmilzt es.)*
Besonderheit bei Formen von *to be*	If I **were** you, I wouldn't use a combination spanner here.

Chronological word list

Videotraining: Englische Aussprache

Perfekte englische Aussprache leicht gemacht: Mit dem Lernprogramm zur englischen Lautschrift können Sie alle Laute einüben. Wählen Sie einfach in der Navigation rechts den entsprechenden Reiter (*Vowels* oder *Consonants*) aus und klicken Sie dann auf das gewünschte phonetische Symbol. Sprechen Sie die Wörter laut nach.

Unter www.klett.de geben Sie bitte den Code unter der Abbildung rechts ein.

n633sn

Abkürzungen und Zeichen

etw. = etwas
Pl. = Plural
jmdn., jmdm. = jemanden, jemandem
sb. = somebody
sth. = something
BE = britisches Englisch
AE = amerikanisches Englisch
◎ = Vokabeln zu den Hörtexten

Module 1 Receiving and checking goods

to store [stɔː] (ein)lagern
warehouse [ˈweəhaʊs] Lager(haus)
transfer point [ˈtrænsfɜː ˌpɔɪnt] Übergabepunkt
goods [gʊdz] Waren
supplier [səˈplaɪə] Lieferant, Zulieferer
contract [ˈkɒntrækt] Vertrag
warehouse worker [ˈweəhaʊs ˌwɜːkə] Lagerarbeiter(in)
to transfer ownership [ˌtrænsfɜːr‿ˈəʊnəʃɪp] Eigentum übertragen
documentation check [ˌdɒkjəmenˈteɪʃn ˌtʃek] Dokumentenüberprüfung
quantitative [ˈkwɒntɪtətɪv] mengenmäßig
quay parking [ˈkiː ˌpɑːkɪŋ] Parken am richtigen Ablageort
to unload [ʌnˈləʊd] entladen, abladen
integration of goods [ɪntɪˌgreɪʃn‿əv ˈgʊdz] Warenaufnahme
stock [stɒk] Lager, Lagerbestand
to be directed [bi dɪˈrektɪd] verwiesen werden
receiving dock [rɪˈsiːvɪŋ ˌdɒk] Empfangsrampe
conveyor belt [kənˈveɪə ˌbelt] Förderband, Transportband
package [ˈpækɪdʒ] Paket
damage [ˈdæmɪdʒ] Beschädigung, Schaden
delivery document [dɪˈlɪvri ˌdɒkjəmənt] Lieferpapier
to take into stock [ˌteɪk‿ɪntə ˈstɒk] auf Lager nehmen
barcode scanner [ˈbɑːkəud ˌskænə] Strichcodeleser

A | People and departments involved in receiving goods

department [dɪˈpɑːtmənt] Abteilung
involved in [ɪnˈvɒlvd‿ɪn] beteiligt an
to take [teɪk] *(hier:)* aufnehmen
condition [kənˈdɪʃn] Zustand
purchasing department [ˈpɜːtʃəsɪŋ dɪˌpɑːtmənt] Einkauf(sabteilung)
receiving staff [rɪˈsiːvɪŋ ˌstɑːf] Personal zuständig für den Wareneingang
receiving department [rɪˈsiːvɪŋ dɪˌpɑːtmənt] Warenannahme

quality department ['kwɒləti dɪˌpɑ:tmənt] Qualitätsabteilung
loss [lɒs] Verlust
transportation company [ˌtrænspɔ:'teɪʃn ˌkʌmpəni] Spedition
to meet [mi:t] *(hier:)* entsprechen
specification [ˌspesɪfɪ'keɪʃn] Angabe, Beschreibung
to place an order [ˌpleɪs‿ən‿'ɔ:də] einen Auftrag erteilen

B | Receiving documentation

carrier ['kærɪə] Frachtführer, Spediteur
delivery note [dɪ'lɪvri ˌnəʊt] Lieferschein
transportation bill [ˌtrænspɔ:'teɪʃn ˌbɪl] Transportschein, -liste
receiving note [rɪ'si:vɪŋ ˌnəʊt] Empfangsbescheinigung
to correspond with [ˌkɒrɪ'spɒnd wɪð] übereinstimmen mit

item ['aɪtəm] Posten, Artikel
to make out [ˌmeɪk‿'aʊt] ausstellen
for the attention of [fə ði‿ə'tənʃn‿əv] zu Händen von
to match [mætʃ] übereinstimmen
invoice number ['ɪnvɔɪs ˌnʌmbə] Rechnungsnummer
order number ['ɔ:də ˌnʌmbə] Auftragsnummer
in case [ɪn 'keɪs] für den Fall
label ['leɪbl] Aufkleber, Aufschrift
to countersign ['kaʊntəsaɪn] gegenzeichnen
signature ['sɪgnətʃə] Unterschrift
to store [stɔ:] (ein)lagern, auf Lager nehmen

visual ['vɪʒuəl] visuell, optisch
dispatch date [dɪ'spætʃ ˌdeɪt] Versanddatum
to arise [ə'raɪz] entstehen

C | Barcode scanners

to display [dɪ'spleɪ] zeigen

Module A Meeting people

confident ['kɒnfɪdənt] sicher, selbstbewusst
appropriate [ə'prəʊpriət] angemessen, passend

A | Saying "hello" and "goodbye" and giving your name

existing [ɪg'zɪstɪŋ] bestehend
trade fair ['treɪd ˌfeə] Messe
job fair ['dʒɒb ˌfeə] Jobmesse

B | Intercultural awareness

politeness [pə'laɪtnəs] Höflichkeit
pleasantry ['plezntri] höfliche Floskel
profitability [ˌprɒfɪtəbɪləti] Rentabilität
to chat [tʃæt] sich unterhalten
health [helθ] Gesundheit
pleasant ['pleznt] angenehm
to waste time [ˌweɪst 'taɪm] Zeit verschwenden
impression [ɪm'preʃn] Eindruck
conference ['kɒnfrəns] Tagung
minutes ['mɪnɪts] Protokoll
polite [pə'laɪt] höflich
usual ['ju:ʒl] gewöhnlich, üblich, normal
upset [ʌp'set] verärgert
stranger ['streɪndʒə] Unbekannte(r)
on the other hand [ɒn ði‿'ʌðə ˌhænd] andererseits
in charge of [ɪn 'tʃɑ:dʒ‿əv] verantwortlich für
cash register ['kæʃ ˌredʒɪstə] Kasse
given name [ˌgɪvn 'neɪm] Vorname
family name [ˌfæmli 'neɪm] Nachname
to intend [ɪn'tend] beabsichtigen

Module 2 Storing and handling goods

to store [stɔ:] (ein)lagern
to handle ['hændl] handhaben
properly ['prɒpli] richtig
warehouse ['weəhaʊs] Lager(haus)
to locate [lə'keɪt] (wieder)finden
to misplace [mɪ'spleɪs] verlegen, an die falsche Stelle setzen
to damage ['dæmɪdʒ] beschädigen
pallet ['pælɪt] Palette
shelf [ʃelf] Regal
bin [bɪn] Behälter
forklift ['fɔ:klɪft] Gabelstapler
to place [pleɪs] platzieren
rack [ræk] Regal
storage system ['stɔ:rɪdʒ ˌsɪstəm] Lagersystem
from the bottom [frəm ðə 'bɒtəm] von unten

A | Storage facilities

storage facilities ['stɔ:rɪdʒ fəˌsɪlətiz] Lagermöglichkeiten
damage ['dæmɪdʒ] Beschädigung, Schaden
to avoid [ə'vɔɪd] vermeiden
crate [kreɪt] Kiste
shelving rack ['ʃelvɪŋ ˌræk] Fachregal
rubber ['rʌbə] Gummi
to palletize ['pælɪtaɪz] palettieren, auf Paletten packen
to wrap [ræp] einwickeln, einpacken, umhüllen
size [saɪz] Größe
bulky ['bʌlki] sperrig, unhandlich, übergroß
tyre ['taɪə] Reifen
apprentice [ə'prentɪs] Auszubildende(r)
steering wheel ['stɪərɪŋ ˌwi:l] Lenkrad
work placement ['wɜ:k ˌpleɪsmənt] Praktikum

warehouse management system [ˌweəhaʊs 'mænɪdʒmənt ˌsɪstəm] Lagerverwaltungssystem
accessories [ək'sesriz] Zubehör
windscreen wiper ['wɪnskri:n ˌwaɪpə] Scheibenwischer
in operation [ɪn‿ɒpr'eɪʃn] in Betrieb

B | Storing products in the right place

condition [kən'dɪʃn] Zustand
humidity [hju:'mɪdəti] Feuchtigkeit
stock [stɒk] Waren
hazardous ['hæzədəs] gefährlich
gas [gæs] Gas
well-ventilated [ˌwel'ventɪleɪtɪd] gut belüftet
safety controlled [ˌseɪfti kən'trəʊld] sicherheitsüberwacht
space [speɪs] Platz, Raum
board [bɔ:d] Brett
dairy product ['deəri ˌprɒdʌkt] Milchprodukt
to spoil [spɔɪl] verderben
liquid chemical [ˌlɪkwɪd 'kemɪkl] flüssige Chemikalie
flammable ['flæməbl] leicht entzündlich
solid ['sɒlɪd] Feststoff
explosive [ɪk'spləʊsɪv] Sprengstoff
mattress ['mætrəs] Matratze
spring [sprɪŋ] Feder
helmet ['helmət] Helm

C | Labelling goods

to label ['leɪbl] etikettieren, beschriften
handling symbol ['hændlɪŋ ˌsɪmbl] Handhabungssymbol
packaging ['pækɪdʒɪŋ] Verpackung(smaterial)
flammable ['flæməbl] leicht entzündlich
fragile ['frædʒaɪl] zerbrechlich
to keep cool [ˌki:p 'ku:l] kühl lagern
to keep dry [ˌki:p 'draɪ] trocken lagern
perfume ['pɜ:fju:m] Parfüm
piano [pi'ænəʊ] Klavier
operating process ['ɒpreɪtɪŋ ˌprəʊses] Arbeitsablauf
to optimize ['ɒptɪmaɪz] optimieren
receipt of stock [rɪˌsi:t‿əv 'stɒk] Wareneingang
return [rɪ'tɜ:n] Rücklieferung, Rücksendung
to monitor ['mɒnɪtə] überwachen, kontrollieren
wirelessly ['waɪələsli] drahtlos
database ['deɪtəbeɪs] Datenbank
to provide [prə'vaɪd] versorgen
cost-efficient [ˌkɒstɪ'fɪʃnt] kostengünstig, wirtschaftlich
costs [kɒsts] Kosten
reliable [rɪ'laɪəbl] zuverlässig
physical inventory [ˌfɪzɪkl‿ɪn'ventri] physische Bestandsaufnahme
shipping [ʃɪpɪŋ] Versand
query ['kwɪəri] (Such-)Anfrage
barcode labelling ['bɑ:kəʊd ˌleɪblɪŋ] Barcode-Etikettierung

Module B Your company

regardless of [rɪ'gɑ:dləs‿əv] ungeachtet, unabhängig von
furniture ['fɜ:nɪtʃə] Möbel
likely ['laɪkli] wahrscheinlich
supplier [sə'plaɪə] Lieferant, Zulieferer
skill [skɪl] Fähigkeit, Fertigkeit
to express [ɪk'spres] zum Ausdruck bringen
grease [gri:s] Fett
ratchet ['rætʃɪt] Knarre
tool [tu:l] Werkzeug

A | The company and its departments

department [dɪ'pɑ:tmənt] Abteilung
to distribute [dɪ'strɪbju:t] vertreiben, verteilen
damaged ['dæmɪdʒd] beschädigt
employee [ɪm'plɔɪi:] Beschäftigte(r), Angestellte(r)

accounts [ə'kaʊnts] Buchhaltung
raw materials [ˌrɔ: mə'tɪəriəlz] Rohstoffe
human resources [ˌhju:mən 'ri:zɔ:sɪz] Personalabteilung
to recruit [rɪ'kru:t] rekrutieren, anstellen
purchasing (department) ['pɜ:tʃəsɪŋ (dɪˌpɑ:tmənt)] Einkauf(sabteilung)
to maintain [meɪn'teɪn] warten, in Stand halten
R&D (Research and Development) [rɪˌsɜ:tʃ‿ən dɪ'veləpmənt] Forschungs- und Entwicklungsabteilung
to develop [dɪ'veləp] entwickeln
in charge of [ɪn 'tʃɑ:dʒ‿əv] zuständig für

to cover ['kʌvə] abdecken, bedecken
headquarters [ˌhed'kwɔ:təz] Hauptsitz
to found [faʊnd] gründen
family-owned [ˌfæmli'əʊnd] in Familienbesitz
manufacturing plant [ˌmænjə'fæktʃərɪŋ ˌplɑ:nt] Produktionsbetrieb
currently ['kʌrəntli] derzeit, zurzeit, momentan
braking system ['breɪkɪŋ ˌsɪstəm] Bremsanlage
internship (AE) ['ɪntɜ:rnʃɪp] Praktikum
device [dɪ'vaɪs] Gerät
cylinder head ['sɪlɪndə ˌhed] Zylinderkopf
to inspect [ɪn'spekt] prüfen
operating system ['ɒpreɪtɪŋ ˌsɪstəm] Betriebssystem
interface ['ɪntəfeɪs] Schnittstelle, Interface

B | Tasks and responsibilities

task [tɑ:sk] Aufgabe
responsibility [rɪˌspɒnsə'bɪləti] Verantwortung
to manufacture [ˌmænjə'fæktʃə] herstellen
to occur [ə'kɜ:] vorkommen
apprenticeship [ə'prentɪsʃɪp] Ausbildung, Lehre
branch [brɑ:nʃ] Niederlassung
precision [prɪ'sɪʒn] Genauigkeit
essential [ɪ'senʃl] wesentlich, unbedingt erforderlich
to drill [drɪl] bohren
to shape [ʃeɪp] formen, fräsen
to polish ['pɒlɪʃ] abschleifen, polieren
to intervene [ˌɪntə'vi:n] einschreiten
to vibrate [vaɪ'breɪt] vibrieren
workpiece ['wɜ:kpi:s] Werkstück
to monitor ['mɒnɪtə] überwachen, kontrollieren, beobachten
to measure ['meʒə] messen
dimension [daɪ'menʃn] Maß, Abmessung

lubricated ['lu:brɪkeɪtɪd] geölt
lubricating oil ['lu:brɪkeɪtɪŋ‿ɔɪl] Schmieröl
generally ['dʒenrəli] normalerweise, im Allgemeinen
shift [ʃɪft] Schicht
to prefer [prɪ'fɜ:] bevorzugen
rarely ['reəli] selten
accuracy ['ækjərəsi] Genauigkeit
to include [ɪn'klu:d] einbeziehen, einschließen
to swap [swɒp] tauschen

C | Organisational structure

to employ [ɪm'plɔɪ] beschäftigen
to support [sə'pɔ:t] unterstützen
to split [splɪt] aufteilen
core area [ˌkɔ: 'eəriə] Kernbereich
to report to [rɪ'pɔ:t tu:] unterstehen
to belong to [bɪ'lɒŋ tu:] gehören zu
experienced [ɪk'spɪəriənst] erfahren
capable ['keɪpəbl] fähig
closely ['kləʊsli] eng

Module 3 Moving goods in the warehouse

robot ['rəʊbɒt] Roboter
conveyor belt [kən'veɪə ˌbelt] Förderband
handling system ['hændlɪŋ ˌsɪstəm] Handhabungssystem
permanently installed [ˌpɜ:mnəntli‿ɪn'stɔ:ld] fest installiert
manually ['mænjʊəlɪ] von Hand, manuell
storage place ['stɔ:rɪdʒ ˌpleɪs] Lagerort, Lagerplatz
light [laɪt] leicht
mechanical handling equipment [məˌkænɪkl 'hændlɪŋ‿ɪˌkwɪpmənt] mechanische Fördervorrichtungen
forklift truck [ˌfɔ:klɪft‿'trʌk] Gabelstapler
lifting cart ['lɪftɪŋ ˌkɑ:t] Hubwagen

A | Automatic and mechanical handling systems

automatic [ˌɔ:tə'mætɪk] automatisch
to store [stɔ:] (ein)lagern
to retrieve [rɪ'tri:v] wiederfinden
efficient [ɪ'fɪʃnt] effizient
reliably [rɪ'laɪəbli] zuverlässig
inflexible [ɪn'fleksəbl] unflexibel

◎ **to agree** [ə'gri:] zustimmen
guided tour [ˌgaɪdɪd 'tʊə] Führung
to improve [ɪm'pru:v] verbessern
to install [ɪn'stɔ:l] installieren
to depend on [dɪ'pend‿ɒn] davon abhängen
chemical warehouse ['kemɪkl ˌweəhaʊs] Lagerhaus für Chemikalien
roller conveyor [ˌrəʊlə kən'veɪə] Rollenbahn
overhead conveyor system [ˌəʊvəhed kən'veɪə ˌsɪstəm] Hängebahnanlage
fashion warehouse ['fæʃn ˌweəhaʊs] Lagerhaus für Modeartikel
production area [prə'dʌkʃn‿eəriə] Fertigungsbereich
economical [ˌi:kə'nɒmɪkl] kostengünstig, wirtschaftlich
to break down [ˌbreɪk‿'daʊn] eine Panne haben
pallet ['pælɪt] Palette
pallet rack ['pælɪt ˌræk] Regalanlage
suitable ['su:təbl] geeignet
to manoeuver [mə'nu:və] manövrieren

item ['aɪtəm] Posten, Artikel
size [saɪz] Größe
to stack [stæk] stapeln
solid ['sɒlɪd] stabil
even ['i:vn] glatt
surface ['sɜ:fɪs] Oberfläche
hazardous ['hæzədəs] gefährlich
carefully ['keəfli] vorsichtig
customer ['kʌstəmə] Kunde, Kundin

B | Manual handling regulations

handling regulation ['hændlɪŋ regjəˌleɪʃn] Handhabungsvorschrift
load [ləʊd] Last
back [bæk] Rücken
knee [ni:] Knie
to cause [kɔ:z] verursachen, auslösen
serious ['sɪərɪəs] ernsthaft
injury ['ɪndʒri] Verletzung
protective clothing [prəˌtektɪv 'kləʊðɪŋ] Sicherheitsbekleidung
to avoid [ə'vɔɪd] vermeiden
to bend [bend] biegen
to lift [lɪft] (hoch)heben
smooth [smu:θ] ruhig
motion ['məʊʃn] Bewegung
clear [klɪə] frei
straight [streɪt] gerade
stable ['steɪbl] stabil
to pick up [ˌpɪk‿'ʌp] aufnehmen
repetitive [rɪ'petətɪv] monoton, sich wiederholend
gas [gæs] Gas
to involve [ɪn'vɒlv] umfassen
suffer with ['sʌfə wɪð] leiden unter
condition [kən'dɪʃn] Bedingung
properly ['prɒpəlɪ] richtig
voice [vɔɪs] Stimm-
to prevent [prɪ'vent] vermeiden

C | Driving a forklift

turn ['tɜ:n] Kurve
obstacle ['ɒbstəkl] Hindernis
horn [hɔ:n] Hupe
to adjust [ə'dʒʌst] einstellen
tyre [taɪə] Reifen
hole [həʊl] Loch
emergency brake [ɪˌmɜ:dʒnsi 'breɪk] Notbremse
loose [lu:s] lose, locker
connection [kə'nekʃn] Verbindung

Module C Telephoning

line [laɪn] *(hier:)* Branche
to fix [fɪks] reparieren
leak [li:k] undichte Stelle
to install [ɪn'stɔ:l] installieren, montieren, anschließen
complaint [kəm'pleɪnt] Beschwerde, Reklamation
order ['ɔ:də] Bestellung, Auftrag
necessary ['nesəsri] nötig, notwendig
delay [dɪ'leɪ] Verspätung, Verzögerung
breakdown ['breɪkdaʊn] Panne, Störung
solution [sə'lu:ʃn] Lösung
confused [kən'fju:zd] verwirrt
crash [kræʃ] Absturz

A | Making and receiving a phone call

meeting ['mi:tɪŋ] Sitzung, Besprechung
country code ['kʌntri ˌkəʊd] Ländervorwahl
area code ['eəriə ˌkəʊd] Vorwahl
extension number [ɪk'stenʃn ˌnʌmbə] Durchwahl
suitable ['su:təbl] geeignet, passend
polite [pə'laɪt] höflich
although [ɔ:l'ðəʊ] obwohl
to remain [rɪ'meɪn] bleiben
request [rɪ'kwest] Bitte
grateful ['greɪtfl] dankbar

whereas [weə'ræz] während
impolite [ˌɪmpə'laɪt] unhöflich

B | Giving information over the phone

valuable ['væljuəbl] *(hier:)* wichtig
figures ['fɪgəz] Nummern, Daten
clearly ['klɪəli] deutlich, klar

confused [kən'fju:zd] verwirrt
to divert [daɪ'vɜ:rt] weiterleiten
extractor fan [ɪk'stræktə fæn] Dunstabzug
hob [hɒb] Kochfeld
diameter [daɪ'æmətə] Durchmesser
socket ['sɒkɪt] Steckdose

Module 4 Picking and consigning goods

to pick [pɪk] entnehmen, kommissionieren
to consign [kən'saɪn] versenden
order picking ['ɔ:də ˌpɪkɪŋ] Kommissionieren, Auftragszusammenstellung
to ship [ʃɪp] versenden, verschiffen
to place an order [ˌpleɪs‿ən‿'ɔ:də] eine Bestellung aufgeben
customer satisfaction [ˌkʌstəmə ˌsætɪs'fækʃn] Kundenzufriedenheit
order ['ɔ:də] Bestellung, Auftrag
lifting cart [lɪftɪŋ ˌkɑ:t] Hubwagen
to load up [ˌləʊd‿'ʌp] beladen, aufladen
pallet rack ['pælɪt ˌræk] Palettenregal
picking list ['pɪkɪŋ ˌlɪst] Kommissionierliste
storage place ['stɔ:rɪdʒ ˌpleɪs] Lagerort
item ['aɪtəm] Artikel, Posten
account [ə'kaʊnt] Konto; Kunde / Kundin; Rechnung
salesperson ['seɪlzˌpɜ:sn] Verkäufer(in)
terms [tɜ:mz] (Liefer-)Bedingungen

A | Order picking systems

picking area ['pɪkɪŋ‿eəriə] Kommissionierbereich
material handling system [məˌtɪəriəl 'hændlɪŋ ˌsɪstəm] Transportanlage
picking bay ['pɪkɪŋ ˌbeɪ] Kommissionierplatz
dispatch [dɪ'spætʃ] Versand

capital expenditure [ˌkæpɪtl‿ ɪk'spendɪtʃə] Investitionsaufwand

B | Order picking methods

labour-intensive [ˌleɪbərɪn'tensɪv] arbeitsintensiv
expense [ɪk'spens] Kosten
sequential order picking [sɪˌkwenʃl‿'ɔ:də ˌpɪkɪŋ] auftragsorientierte, serielle Kommissionierung
parallel order picking [ˌpærəlel‿'ɔ:də ˌpɪkɪŋ] auftragsorientierte, parallele Kommissionierung
parallel sequential picking [ˌpærəlel sɪ'kwenʃl ˌpɪkɪŋ] serienorientierte, parallele Kommissionierung
to combine [kəm'baɪn] zusammenführen
sub-series ['sʌbˌsɪəri:z] Unterserien
simultaneously [ˌsɪml'teɪniəsli] gleichzeitig
to sort [sɔ:t] sortieren
partial order [ˌpɑ:ʃl‿'ɔ:də] Teilauftrag
efficiency [ɪ'fɪʃnsi] Effizienz
significantly [sɪg'nɪfɪkntli] bedeutend
operating costs ['ɒpreɪtɪŋ ˌkɒsts] laufende Kosten
demand [dɪ'mɑ:nd] Nachfrage
routing method ['ru:tɪŋ ˌmeθəd] elektronisches System zur Übermittlung von Aufträgen
measurement ['meʒəmənt] Messwert, Messung
to store [stɔ:] (ein)lagern

C | Storage systems

storage system ['stɔ:rɪdʒ ˌsɪstəm] Lagersystem
perishables ['perɪʃəblz] (leicht) verderbliche Ware(n)

Module D Written communication

essential [ɪ'senʃl] sehr wichtig
workshop ['wɜ:kʃɒp] Werkstatt
efficiently [ɪ'fɪʃntli] effizient
necessary ['nesəsri] nötig, notwendig
enquiry [ɪn'kwaɪəri] Anfrage
promptly ['prɒmtli] sofort
offer ['ɒfə] Angebot
order ['ɔ:də] Bestellung
to replace [rɪ'pleɪs] ersetzen
lesser ['lesə] geringer
advantage [əd'vɑ:ntɪdʒ] Vorteil
disadvantage [ˌdɪsəd'vɑ:ntɪdʒ] Nachteil
confidential [ˌkɒnfɪ'denʃl] vertraulich
time-consuming ['taɪmkənˌsju:mɪŋ] zeitraubend

reliable [rɪˈlaɪəbl] zuverlässig
misunderstanding [ˌmɪsʌndəˈstændɪŋ] Missverständnis

A | Enquiries

enquiry [ɪnˈkwaɪəri] Anfrage
car mechanic [ˈkɑː mɪˌkænɪk] Automechaniker(in)
appropriate [əˈprəʊpriət] angemessen, passend
salutation [ˌsæljəˈteɪʃn] *(Brief:)* Anrede
supplier [səˈplaɪə] Lieferant, Zulieferer
subject line [ˈsʌbdʒɪkt ˌlaɪn] *(Brief:)* Betreffzeile
bonnet (BE) [ˈbɒnɪt] Motorhaube
family-run [ˌfæmliˈrʌn] in Familienbesitz, familiengeführt
to expand [ɪkˈspænd] erweitern, vergrößern
catalogue [ˈkætəlɒg] Katalog
discount [ˈdɪskaʊnt] Rabatt, Preisnachlass
terms of payment [ˌtɜːmz‿əv ˈpeɪmənt] Zahlungsbedingungen
delivery times [dɪˈlɪvri ˌtaɪmz] Lieferzeiten
sample [ˈsæmpl] Muster
closing phrase [ˈkləʊzɪŋ ˌfreɪz] Schlussworte
complimentary close [ˌkɒmplɪmentri ˈkləʊz] Grußformel (am Briefende)
to recommend [ˌrekəˈmend] empfehlen
cost estimate [ˈkɒst‿ˌestɪmət] Kostenvoranschlag
configure [kənˈfɪgə] konfigurieren
to appreciate [əˈpriːʃieɪt] etw. (wert)schätzen
supply from stock [səˌplaɪ frəm ˈstɒk] ab Lager liefern

B | Offers

bank transfer [ˈbæŋk ˌtrænsfɜː] Banküberweisung
working day [ˌwɜːkɪŋ ˈdeɪ] Werktag
attachment [əˈtætʃmənt] Anhang
stock [stɒk] Bestand, Vorrat
to require [rɪˈkwaɪə] benötigen
ratchet [ˈrætʃɪt] Knarre, Ratsche
socket [ˈsɒkɪt] Stecknuss
(adjustable) wrench [əˌdʒʌstəbl ˈrenʃ] (verstellbarer) Schraubenschlüssel
screwdriver [ˈskruːˌdraɪvə] Schraubendreher
to dispatch [dɪˈspætʃ] versenden, verschicken
DIY (Do-it-yourself) [ˌdiːaɪˈwaɪ] Heimwerken

C | Orders

sum [sʌm] Betrag
consignment [kənˈsaɪnmənt] Lieferung, Sendung
torque wrench [ˈtɔːk ˌrenʃ] Drehmomentschlüssel

Module 5 Packing goods

to pack [pæk] (ver)packen
packing [ˈpækɪŋ] Verpacken, Verpackung
storage [ˈstɔːrɪdʒ] Lager(haltung)
purpose [ˈpɜːpəs] (Verwendungs-)Zweck
undamaged [ʌnˈdæmɪdʒd] unbeschädigt
to stock [stɒk] (ein)lagern
wooden crate [ˌwʊdn ˈkreɪt] Holzkiste
handling symbol [ˈhændlɪŋ ˌsɪmbl] Handhabungssymbol
cardboard box [ˌkɑːdbɔːd ˈbɒks] Pappkarton
stack [stæk] Stapel
freight container [ˈfreɪt kənˌteɪnə] Frachtcontainer
dock [dɒk] Dock, Kai, Hafenbecken
strap [stræp] Band, Riemen
to label [ˈleɪbl] etikettieren, kennzeichnen, beschriften
to keep [kiːp] (be)halten
handle with care [ˌhændl wɪð ˈkeə] Vorsicht zerbrechlich
this side up [ˌðɪs saɪd‿ˈʌp] diese Seite nach oben
arrow [ˈærəʊ] Pfeil

A | Adequate packaging

packaging [ˈpækɪdʒɪŋ] Verpackung(smaterial)
to protect [prəˈtekt] schützen
bale [beɪl] Ballen
barrel [ˈbærl] Fass
drum [drʌm] Trommel, Behälter
one-way pallet [ˌwʌnweɪ ˈpælɪt] Einwegpalette
intern (AE) [ˈɪntɜːn] Praktikant(in)

humidity [hjuːˈmɪdəti] Feuchtigkeit
fragile [ˈfrædʒaɪl] zerbrechlich
to drop [drɒp] fallen lassen
to waste [weɪst] verschwenden
space [speɪs] Platz, Raum

B | Packing materials

bubble wrap [ˈbʌbl ˌræp] Luftpolsterfolie
foam peanut [ˌfəʊm ˈpiːnʌt] Schaumstofferdnuss
pressure [ˈpreʃə] Druck
adhesive tape [ədˌhiːsɪv ˈteɪp] Klebeband
packing paper [ˈpækɪŋ ˌpeɪpə] Packpapier
polystyrene [ˌpɒlɪˈstaɪriːn] Styropor
rope [rəʊp] Band
to fix [fɪks] befestigen, fixieren
lightweight [ˈlaɪtweɪt] leicht(gewichtig)

cushioning ['kʌʃnɪŋ] Polsterung
layer ['leɪə] Schicht
bungee cord ['bʌndʒi ˌkɔ:d] Gummiband
to secure [sɪ'kjʊə] (ab)sichern, schützen

C | Handling signs

to load [ləʊd] (be)laden
hook [hʊk] Haken
centre of gravity [ˌsentər‿əv 'grævəti] Schwerpunkt
blade [bleɪd] Klinge
handtruck ['hæntrʌk] Steckkarren
stacking limitation ['stækɪŋ lɪmɪˌteɪʃn] maximale Stapellast

D | Loading goods

safety rule ['seɪfti ˌru:l] Sicherheitsvorschrift
to underestimate [ˌʌndər'estɪmeɪt] unterschätzen
means of transport [ˌmi:nz‿əv 'trænspɔ:t] Transportmittel
loading dock ['ləʊdɪŋ ˌdɒk] Laderampe
slippery ['slɪpri] rutschig
fall protection ['fɔ:l prəˌtekʃn] Absturzsicherung
manoeuvring [mə'nu:vrɪŋ] Manövrieren
instruction [ɪn'strʌkʃn] Anweisung
load space ['ləʊd ˌspeɪs] Ladefläche
to overload [ˌəʊvl'əʊd] überladen
lashing ['læʃɪŋ] Verschnürung

Module E Applications

to sign [saɪn] unterschreiben
application [ˌæplɪ'keɪʃn] Bewerbung
opportunity [ˌɒpə'tju:nəti] Möglichkeit
to decide [dɪ'saɪd] sich entscheiden
branch [brɑ:nʃ] Niederlassung
advert ['ædvɜ:t] Anzeige
letter of application [ˌletər‿əv‿ˌæplɪ'keɪʃn] Bewerbungsschreiben
CV (curriculum vitae) [ˌsi:'vi:, kəˌrɪkjələm 'vi:taɪ] Lebenslauf
job interview ['dʒɒb‿ˌɪntəvju:] Vorstellungsgespräch
employment contract [ɪm'plɔɪmənt ˌkɒntrækt] Arbeitsvertrag
to invite [ɪn'vaɪt] einladen
skill [skɪl] Fähigkeit
industry ['ɪndəstri] *(hier:)* Branche
hard-working [ˌhɑ:d'wɜ:kɪŋ] fleißig

A | Job advertisements

recently ['ri:sntli] kürzlich
willing to learn [ˌwɪlɪŋ tə 'lɜ:n] lernbereit, lernwillig
responsible [rɪ'spɒnsəbl] verantwortlich
punctual ['pʌŋktʃuəl] pünktlich
pleasant ['pleznt] angenehm, sympathisch
working atmosphere [ˌwɜ:kɪŋ‿'ætməsfɪə] Arbeitsklima
valid ['vælɪd] gültig
troubleshooting ['trʌblˌʃu:tɪŋ] Fehlersuche
to maintain [meɪn'teɪn] bewahren
leading ['li:dɪŋ] führend
supplier [sə'plaɪə] Lieferant, Zulieferer
vacancy ['veɪknsi] freie Stelle
fault [fɒlt] Fehler
assembly [ə'sembli] Montage
summary ['sʌmri] Zusammenfassung

B | Letter of application

letter of application [ˌletər‿əv‿ˌæplɪ'keɪʃn] Bewerbungsschreiben
internship (AE) ['ɪntɜ:rnʃɪp] Praktikum
theoretical [θɪə'retɪkl] theoretisch
to gain [geɪn] *(hier:)* sammeln
reliable [rɪ'laɪəbl] zuverlässig
to consider [kən'sɪdə] betrachten
to require [rɪ'kwaɪə] benötigen

C | The CV

advice [əd'vaɪs] Rat
tip [tɪp] Tipp, Hinweis
to highlight ['haɪlaɪt] betonen
strength [streŋθ] Stärke
achievement [ə'tʃi:vmənt] Leistung
supervisor ['su:pəvaɪzə] Leiter(in), Kontrolleur(in)
truth [tru:θ] Wahrheit
embarrassing [ɪm'bærəsɪŋ] peinlich
to spell [spel] buchstabieren
grateful ['greɪtfl] dankbar

Module 6 Handling dangerous goods

to handle ['hændl] umgehen mit, handhaben
solid ['sɒlɪd] Feststoff
liquid ['lɪkwɪd] Flüssigkeit
property ['prɒpəti] (Grund-)Besitz, Eigentum

environment [ɪn'vaɪrnmənt] Umwelt
hazardous goods [ˌhæzədəs 'gʊdz] Gefahrengut
protective clothing [prəˌtektɪv 'kləʊðɪŋ] Schutzkleidung
safety precaution ['seɪfti prɪˌkɔ:ʃn] Sicherheitsvorkehrung
packaging ['pækɪdʒɪŋ] Verpackung(smaterial)
to load [ləʊd] (ver)laden
securely [sɪ'kjʊəli] sicher
glove [glʌv] Handschuh
goggles ['gɒglz] Schutzbrille
mask [mɑ:sk] Maske
protective overall [prəˌtektɪv‿'əʊvrɔ:l] Schutzanzug
safety boots ['seɪfti ˌbu:ts] Sicherheitsschuhe
to breathe (in) [ˌbri:ð‿'ɪn] (ein)atmen
to protect [prə'tekt] schützen, bewahren

A | Safety precautions and warning signs

acid ['æsɪd] Säure
forklift truck [ˌfɔ:klɪft 'trʌk] Gabelstapler
nail [neɪl] Nagel
detergent [dɪ'tɜ:dʒnt] Reinigungsmittel
irritant ['ɪrɪtnt] reizend, reizauslösend
substance ['sʌbstns] Substanz
pesticide ['pestɪsaɪd] Pestizid
propane ['prəʊpeɪn] Propan(gas)
compressed [kəm'prest] komprimiert, verdichtet
corrosive [kə'rəʊsɪv] ätzend
explosive [ɪk'spləʊsɪv] Sprengstoff
poison ['pɔɪzn] Gift

B | Packing dangerous goods

to resist [rɪ'zɪst] widerstehen, standhalten
height [haɪt] Höhe
adhesive tape [əd'hi:sɪv ˌteɪp] Klebeband
barrel ['bærl] Fass, Tonne
cardboard box [ˌkɑ:dbɔ:d 'bɒks] Pappkarton
to label [leɪbl] etikettieren, kennzeichnen, beschriften
to leak out [ˌli:k‿'aʊt] auslaufen
safety can ['seɪfti ˌkæn] Sicherheitsflasche, -kanister
number label ['nʌmbə ˌleɪbl] Kennzahlaufkleber
prohibition sign [ˌprəʊɪ'bɪʃn ˌsaɪn] Verbotsschild
mandatory sign ['mændətri ˌsaɪn] Gebotsschild
emergency sign [ɪ'mɜ:dʒnsi ˌsaɪn] Notfallschild
fire safety sign [ˌfaɪə 'seɪfti ˌsaɪn] Brandschutzschild

C | Loading hazardous goods

guideline ['gaɪdlaɪn] Richtlinie
to unload [ʌn'ləʊd] entladen
means of transport [ˌmi:nz‿əv 'trænspɔ:t] Transportmittel
carrier ['kæriə] Frachtführer, Transportunternehmen
pallet [pælɪt] Palette
cargo (Pl. cargoes) ['kɑ:gəʊ] Ladung, Fracht
securing means [sɪ'kjʊərɪŋ ˌmi:nz] sichernde Maßnahme(n)
lumber ['lʌmbə] Holz
bar [bɑ:] Stange, Bügel, Leiste
lashing ['læʃɪŋ] Verschnürung
to ensure [ɪn'ʃɔ:] gewährleisten, sicherstellen
loading dock ['ləʊdɪŋ ˌdɒk] Laderampe
slippery ['slɪpri] rutschig
to roll off [ˌrəʊl‿'ɒf] wegrollen
fall protection ['fɔ:l prəˌtekʃn] Fallschutz

Module F Socialising

relationship [rɪ'leɪʃnʃɪp] Beziehung

A | Small talk

subsidiary [səb'sɪdɪəri] Tochtergesellschaft
trainee [ˌtreɪ'ni:] Auszubildende(r)
appropriate [ə'prəʊpriət] angemessen, passend

B | Small talk in business

to dismiss [dɪ'smɪs] nicht beachten
common ground [ˌkɒmən 'graʊnd] gemeinsame Basis
trivial ['trɪviəl] unwichtig
uneasiness [ʌn'i:zinəs] Unbehagen
tension ['tenʃn] Spannung
to avoid [ə'vɔɪd] vermeiden
awkward ['ɔ:kwəd] peinlich, unangenehm

C | Eating out

well-done [ˌwel'dʌn] (Steak) gut durchgebraten
pork [pɔ:k] Schweinefleisch
side order ['saɪd‿ɔ:də] Beilage
bill [bɪl] Rechnung
game [geɪm] *(hier:)* Wild
dessert [dɪ'zɜ:t] Nachtisch, Nachspeise
fork [fɔ:k] Gabel
main dish [ˌmeɪn 'dɪʃ] Hauptgericht

beef [bi:f] Rindfleisch
poultry ['pəʊltri] Geflügel
starter ['stɑ:tə] Vorspeise
tip [tɪp] Trinkgeld

Module 7 Shipping goods

to ship [ʃɪp] versenden, verschiffen
schedule ['ʃedju:l] Zeitplan
destination [ˌdestɪ'neɪʃn] Zielort, Bestimmungsort
to deliver [dɪ'lɪvə] liefern, zustellen
destination port [ˌdestɪ'neɪʃn ˌpɔ:t] Bestimmungshafen
loading dock ['ləʊdɪŋ ˌdɒk] Ladedock
to store [stɔ:] (ein)lagern
to load [ləʊd] (ver)laden
means of transport [mi:nz‿əv 'trænspɔ:t] Transportmittel

A | Different means of transport

perishable ['perɪʃəbl] (leicht) verderblich
efficiently [ɪ'fɪʃntli] effizient
according to [ə'kɔ:dɪŋ tə] nach, gemäß
carrier ['kæriə] Beförderungsunternehmen, Frachtführer
freight [freɪt] Fracht
environmentally friendly [ɪnˌvaɪrnˌmentli 'frendli] umweltfreundlich
refrigerator wagon [rɪ'frɪdʒreɪtə ˌwægən] Kühlwaggon
hazardous ['hæzədəs] gefährlich
urgent ['ɜ:dʒnt] dringend, eilig
waterway ['wɔ:təweɪ] Wasserweg
bulky ['bʌlki] Sperr-, sperrig
seaworthy ['si:ˌwɜ:ði] seefest
packing ['pækɪŋ] Versandverpackung
to protect [prə'tekt] (be)schützen
low-value [ˌləʊ'vælju:] geringwertig
liquid ['lɪkwɪd] Flüssigkeit
air freight ['eəˌfreɪt] Luftfracht
spare part [ˌspeə 'pɑ:t] Ersatzteil
reliable [rɪ'laɪəbl] zuverlässig

B | Organising transportation

to reach an agreement [ri:tʃ‿ən‿ə'gri:mənt] eine Vereinbarung treffen
consignment [kən'saɪnmənt] Warensendung
fragile ['frædʒaɪl] zerbrechlich
to label ['leɪbl] etikettieren, kennzeichnen, beschriften
overseas [ˌəʊvə'si:z] (nach / in) Übersee
warehouse ['weəhaʊs] Lager(haus)
storeman ['stɔ:mən] Lagerist, Lagerverwalter
environmental costs [ɪnˌvaɪrnˌmentl 'kɒsts] Umweltkosten
cause [kɔ:z] Ursache
disaster [dɪ'zɑ:stə] Katastrophe, Unglück
to hit [hɪt] treffen, aufprallen
flood [flʌd] Flut, Überflutung
drought [draʊt] Dürre
oil spill ['ɔɪl ˌspɪl] Ölkatastrophe
on time [ˌɒn 'taɪm] pünktlich

C | Documentation in foreign trade

foreign trade [ˌfɒrɪn 'treɪd] Außenhandel
indemnity [ɪn'demnəti] Schadenersatz
inspection [ɪn'spekʃn] Prüfung, Kontrolle
terms of delivery [ˌtɜ:mz‿əv dɪ'lɪvri] Lieferbedingungen
contract ['kɒntrækt] Vertrag
to bear [beə] tragen
invoice ['ɪnvɔɪs] Rechnung
to issue ['ɪʃu:] ausstellen, anfertigen
air waybill ['eə ˌweɪbɪl] Luftfrachtbrief
bill of lading [ˌbɪl‿əv 'leɪdɪŋ] Konnossement
certificate of origin [səˌtɪfɪkət‿əv 'ɒrɪdʒɪn] Ursprungszeugnis
to sign [saɪn] unterschreiben, unterzeichnen
commercial invoice [kəˌmɜ:ʃl‿'ɪnvɔɪs] Handelsrechnung
insurance certificate [ɪn'ʃʊərns səˌtɪfɪkət] Versicherungspolice
packing list ['pækɪŋ ˌlɪst] Packliste
imperial measurement [ɪmˌpɪəriəl 'meʒəmənt] *Messung im britischen System der Maße und Gewichte*
metric measurement [ˌmetrɪk 'meʒəmənt] *Messung im metrischen System der Maße und Gewichte*

Module G Presentations

required [rɪ'kwaɪəd] erforderlich, verlangt, erwünscht
service ['sɜ:vɪs] Dienstleistung
positional sketch [pəˌzɪʃnl 'sketʃ] Technologieschema
to develop [dɪ'veləp] entwickeln

to improve [ɪm'pru:v] besser werden, sich verbessern
meeting ['mi:tɪŋ] Sitzung, Besprechung
graph [grɑ:f] Diagramm
chart [tʃɑ:t] Schaubild, Diagramm
preparation [ˌprepr'eɪʃn] Vorbereitung
to explain [ɪk'spleɪn] erklären
sales pitch ['seɪlz ˌpɪtʃ] Verkaufspräsentation
reason ['ri:zn] Grund

A | Preparing a presentation

audience ['ɔ:diəns] Zuhörer (Pl.), Publikum
body language ['bɒdi ˌlæŋgwɪdʒ] Körpersprache
handout ['hændaʊt] Informationsblatt
to prepare [prɪ'peə] vorbereiten
visual aids [ˌvɪʒuəl‿'eɪdz] Anschauungsmaterial, visuelle Hilfen
to describe [dɪ'skraɪb] beschreiben
summary ['sʌmri] Zusammenfassung
overview ['əʊvəvju:] Überblick
to reinforce [ˌri:ɪn'fɔ:s] verstärken, betonen
guidelines ['gaɪdlaɪnz] Leitlinien

B | Describing materials and products

sturdy ['stɜ:di] robust
shiny ['ʃaɪni] glänzend
robust [rə'bʌst] stabil
state-of-the-art [ˌsteɪt‿əv ðiˈ‿ɑ:t] auf dem neuesten Stand (der Technik)
user-friendly [ˌju:zə'frendli] benutzerfreundlich
reliable [rɪ'laɪəbl] zuverlässig
hand-crafted [ˌhæn'krɑ:ftɪd] handgefertigt

C | Delivering a presentation

carpenter ['kɑ:pɪntə] Tischler(in), Zimmerer, Zimmerin
furniture ['fɜ:nɪtʃə] Möbel
trade show ['treɪd ʃəʊ] Messe
lounger ['laʊndʒə] Liegesessel
softwood ['sɒftˌwʊd] Weichholz
timber ['tɪmbə] Holz, Bauholz
joiner ['dʒɔɪnə] Tischler(in), Schreiner(in)
convenience [kənˌvi:niəns] Zweckmäßigkeit, Bequemlichkeit
varnish ['vɑ:nɪʃ] Lack
durable ['djʊərəbl] haltbar
polyurethane coating [ˌpɒlɪˌjʊərəθeɪn 'kəʊtɪŋ] Polyurethanbeschichtung

Module 8 Waste disposal and the environment

waste disposal [ˌweɪst dɪ'spəʊzl] Müll- / Abfallentsorgung
environmental awareness [ɪnˌvaɪrnˌmentl‿ə'weənəs] Umweltbewusstsein
issue ['ɪʃu:] Thema
to protect [prə'tekt] schützen, bewahren
to improve [ɪm'pru:v] verbessern
waste legislation ['weɪst ledʒɪˌsleɪʃn] Abfallgesetzgebung
to handle ['hændl] handhaben, umgehen
European Community (EU) [ˌjʊərəpi:ən kə'mju:nəti, ˌi:'ju:] Europäische Gemeinschaft
industrial waste [ɪnˌdʌstriəl 'weɪst] Industrieabfall
can [kæn] Dose
recycling plant [ˌri:'saɪklɪŋ ˌplɑ:nt] Recyclinganlage
to label ['leɪbl] etikettieren, kennzeichnen, beschriften
environmentally friendly [ɪnˌvaɪrnˌmentli 'frendli] umweltfreundlich
bin [bɪn] Behälter
green dot [ˌgri:n 'dɒt] Grüner Punkt
packaging material ['pækɪdʒɪŋ məˌtɪəriəl] Verpackungsmaterial
household waste [ˌhaʊshəʊld 'weɪst] Hausmüll

A | Waste management

landfill ['lændfɪl] Mülldeponie
to avoid [ə'vɔɪd] vermeiden
to deal (with) ['di:l wɪð] umgehen (mit)
to dispose (of) [dɪ'spəʊz‿əv] entsorgen
environmental impact [ɪnˌvaɪrnˌmentl‿'ɪmpækt] Umweltauswirkung
means of transport [ˌmi:nz‿əv 'trænspɔ:t] Transportmittel
waste disposal firm [ˌweɪst dɪ'spəʊzl ˌfɜ:m] Entsorgungsunternehmen
head storewoman [ˌhed 'stɔ:wʊmən] Lagerleiterin
economic cycle [ˌi:kənɒmɪk 'saɪkl] Wirtschaftskreislauf

vocational school [və'keɪʃnl ˌsku:l] Berufsschule

one-way packaging [ˌwʌnweɪ 'pækɪdʒɪŋ] Einwegverpackung
to pass [pɑ:s] (ein Gesetz) verabschieden
packaging law ['pækɪdʒɪŋ ˌlɔ:] Verpackungsverordnung

to force [fɔːs] zwingen
licence fee [ˈlaɪsns ˌfiː] Lizenzgebühr
waste collection vehicle [ˌweɪst kəˈlekʃn ˌvɪəkl] Müllfahrzeug
multi-way packaging [ˌmʌltɪweɪ ˈpækɪdʒɪŋ] Mehrwegverpackung
supplier [səˈplaɪə] Lieferant, Zulieferer
returnable system [rɪˈtɜːnəbl ˌsɪstəm] Rücknahmesystem
operator [ˈɒpreɪtə] Betreiber(in)
to rent [rent] verleihen
byproduct [ˈbaɪˌprɒdʌkt] Nebenprodukt
depot [ˈdepəʊ] Auslieferungslager

B | EU waste legislation

directive [dɪˈrektɪv] Richtlinie
hazardous [ˈhæzədəs] gefährlich
member state [ˌmembə ˈsteɪt] Mitgliedsstaat
to cooperate [kəʊˈɒpreɪt] zusammenarbeiten
facility [fəˈsɪləti] Anlage
in line with [ɪn ˈlaɪn wɪð] in Übereinstimmung mit, in Einklang mit
regulation [ˌregjəˈleɪʃn] Vorschrift, Bestimmung
in order of priority [ɪn‿ɔːdər‿əv praɪˈɒrəti] nach Priorität

C | Environmental awareness

pollution [pəˌluːʃn] Verschmutzung
engine [ˈendʒɪn] Maschine, Motor
to leak [liːk] auslaufen, entweichen
black water [ˈblæk ˌwɔːtə] Schwarzwasser
sewage [ˈsuːɪdʒ] Abwasser
grey water [ˈgreɪ ˌwɔːtə] Grauwasser
solid waste [ˌsɒlɪd ˈweɪst] Feststoffabfall
to play down [ˌpleɪ ˈdaʊn] herunterspielen
noise pollution [ˈnɔɪz pəˌluːʃn] Lärmbelästigung
sound [saʊnd] Ton, Klang, Geräusch
collision [kəˈlɪʒn] Zusammenstoß
to charge with [ˈtʃɑːdʒ wɪð] verklagen, belasten
violation [ˌvaɪəˈleɪʃn] Verstoß

Module H Dealing with customers

to deal with [ˈdiːl wɪð] umgehen mit, sich befassen mit
customer [ˈkʌstəmə] Kunde, Kundin
success [səkˈses] Erfolg
appointment [əˈpɔɪntmənt] Termin
enquiry [ɪnˈkwaɪəri] Anfrage
complaint [kəmˈpleɪnt] Beschwerde
essential [ɪˈsenʃl] sehr wichtig
builder [ˈbɪldə] Bauunternehmer(in)
building site [ˈbɪldɪŋ ˌsaɪt] Baustelle
to explain [ɪkˈspleɪn] erklären

A | Complaints

solution [səˈluːʃn] Lösung
delay [dɪˈleɪ] Verzögerung, Verspätung
price reduction [ˈpraɪs rɪˌdʌkʃn] Preisnachlass
faulty [ˈfɒlti] fehlerhaft, defekt, mangelhaft
damaged [ˈdæmɪdʒd] beschädigt
unsatisfactory [ʌnˌsætɪsˈfæktri] unbefriedigend, ungenügend, unzureichend
to replace [rɪˈpleɪs] ersetzen
air freight [ˈeə ˌfreɪt] Luftfracht
surplus [ˈsɜːpləs] überschüssig
credit note [ˈkredɪt ˌnəʊt] Gutschrift
specific [spəˈsɪfɪk] bestimmt, spezifisch

access [ˈækses] Zugang
to log on [ˌlɒg‿ˈɒn] sich anmelden, sich einwählen
migration [maɪˈgreɪʃn] *(hier:)* Umstellung
redo [ˌriːˈduː] noch einmal machen
to look into sth. [ˌlʊk‿ˈɪntə] einer Sache nachgehen

technician [tekˈnɪʃn] Techniker(in)
plumbing and heating [ˌplʌmɪŋ‿ənd ˈhiːtɪŋ] Heizung und Sanitär

B | Customer service

upset [ʌpˈset] verärgert
to avoid [əˈvɔɪd] vermeiden
argument [ˈɑːgjəmənt] Streit, Auseinandersetzung
to calm sb. [kɑːm] jmdn. beruhigen
to reassure [ˌriːəˈʃʊə] beruhigen
patient [ˈpeɪʃnt] geduldig
to solve [sɒlv] lösen
frame of mind [ˌfreɪm‿əv ˈmaɪnd] geistige Verfassung
furious [ˈfjʊəriəs] wütend
to affect [əˈfekt] Einfluss nehmen auf
mood [muːd] Laune
to blame sb. / sth. for sth. [bleɪm] jmdm. / etw. die Schuld an etw. geben, jmdn. verantwortlich machen
excuse [ɪkˈskjuːs] Ausrede

Alphabetical word list

A

access Zugang 69
accessories Zubehör 17
according to nach, gemäß 57
account Konto; Kunde / Kundin; Rechnung 32
accounts Buchhaltung 21
accuracy Genauigkeit 23
achievement Leistung 47
acid Säure 49
adhesive tape Klebeband 42, 50
to adjust einstellen 27
advantage Vorteil 36
advert Anzeige 44
advice Rat 47
to affect Einfluss nehmen auf 71
to agree zustimmen 25
air freight Luftfracht 57, 69
air waybill Luftfrachtbrief 59
although obwohl 30
application Bewerbung 44
appointment Termin 68
to appreciate (wert)schätzen 37
apprentice Auszubildende(r) 17
apprenticeship Ausbildung, Lehre 22
appropriate angemessen, passend 12
area code Vorwahl 29
argument Streit, Auseinandersetzung 71
to arise entstehen 10
arrow Pfeil 40
assembly Montage 45
attachment Anhang 38
audience Zuhörer (Pl.), Publikum 61
automatic automatisch 25
to avoid vermeiden 65
awkward peinlich, unangenehm 54

B

back Rücken 26
bale Ballen 41
bank transfer Banküberweisung 38
bar Stange, Bügel, Leiste 51
barcode labelling Barcode-Etikettierung 19
barcode scanner Strichcodeleser 8
barrel Fass 41
to bear tragen 59
to be directed verwiesen werden 8
beef Rindfleisch 55
to belong to gehören zu 23
to bend biegen 26
bill Rechnung 55
bill of lading Konnossement 59
bin Behälter 64
black water Schwarzwasser 67
blade Klinge 43
to blame sb. / sth. for sth. jmdm. / etw. die Schuld an etw. geben, jmdn. verantwortlich machen 71
board Brett 18
body language Körpersprache 61
bonnet (BE) Motorhaube 37
braking system Bremsanlage 21
branch Niederlassung 44
breakdown Panne, Störung 28
to break down eine Panne haben 25
to breathe (in) (ein)atmen 48
bubble wrap Luftpolsterfolie 42
builder Bauunternehmer(in) 68
building site Baustelle 68
bulky Sperr-, sperrig 57
bungee cord Gummiband 42
byproduct Nebenprodukt 65

C

to calm sb. jmdn. beruhigen 71
can Dose 64
capable fähig 23
capital expenditure Investitionsaufwand 33
cardboard box Pappkarton 40
carefully vorsichtig 25
cargo (Pl. cargoes) Ladung, Fracht 51
car mechanic Automechaniker(in) 37
carpenter Tischler(in), Zimmerer, Zimmerin 63
carrier Spediteur, Frachtführer 10, 51, 57
cash register Kasse 15
catalogue Katalog 37
cause Ursache 58
to cause verursachen, auslösen 26
centre of gravity Schwerpunkt 43
certificate of origin Ursprungszeugnis 59
to charge with verklagen, belasten
chart Schaubild, Diagramm 60
to chat sich unterhalten 15
chemical warehouse Lagerhaus für Chemikalien 25
clear frei 26
clearly deutlich, klar 31
closely eng 23
closing phrase Schlussworte 37
collision Zusammenstoß 67
to combine zusammenführen, verbinden 34
commercial invoice Handelsrechnung 59
common ground gemeinsame Basis 54
complaint Beschwerde 68
complimentary close Grußformel (am Briefende) 37
compressed komprimiert, verdichtet 49
condition Zustand 9
conference Tagung 15
confident sicher, selbstbewusst 12
confidential vertraulich 36
configure konfigurieren 37
confused verwirrt 28, 31
connection Verbindung 27
to consider betrachten 46
to consign versenden 32
consignment Lieferung, Sendung 3
contract Vertrag 8
convenience Zweckmäßigkeit, Bequemlichkeit 63

E

F

from the bottom von unten 16
furious wütend 71
furniture Möbel 20

G

to gain *(hier:)* sammeln 46
game *(hier:)* Wild 55
gas Gas 26
generally normalerweise, im Allgemeinen 22
given name Vorname 15
glove Handschuh 48
goggles Schutzbrille 48
goods Waren 8
graph Diagramm 60
grateful dankbar 30
grease Fett 20
grey water Grauwasser 67
guided tour Führung 25
guideline Richtlinie, Leitlinie 51, 61

H

hand-crafted handgefertigt 62
to handle handhaben, umgehen 16, 64
handle with care Vorsicht zerbrechlich 40
handling regulation Handhabungsvorschrift 26
handling symbol Handhabungssymbol 40
handling system Handhabungssystem 24
handout Informationsblatt 61
handtruck Steckkarren 43
hard-working fleißig 44
hazardous gefährlich 57
hazardous goods Gefahrengut 48
headquarters Hauptsitz 21
head storewoman Lagerleiterin 65
health Gesundheit 15
height Höhe 50
helmet Helm 18
to highlight betonen 47
to hit treffen, aufprallen 58
hob Kochfeld
hole Loch 27
hook Haken 43
horn Hupe 27
household waste Hausmüll 64
human resources Personalabteilung 21
humidity Feuchtigkeit 41

I

imperial measurement *Messung im britischen System der Maße und Gewichte* 59
impolite unhöflich 30
impression Eindruck 15
to improve verbessern 64
in case für den Fall 10
in charge of verantwortlich für 15
to include einbeziehen, einschließen 23
indemnity Schadenersatz 59
industrial waste Industrieabfall 64
industry *(hier:)* Branche 44
inflexible unflexibel 25
injury Verletzung 26
in line with in Übereinstimmung mit, in Einklang mit 67
in operation in Betrieb 17
in order of priority nach Priorität 67
to inspect prüfen 21
inspection Prüfung, Kontrolle 59
to install installieren, montieren, anschließen 28
instruction Anweisung 43
insurance certificate Versicherungspolice 59
integration of goods Warenaufnahme 8
to intend beabsichtigen 15
interface Schnittstelle, Interface 21
intern (AE) Praktikant(in) 41
internship (AE) Praktikum 21
to intervene einschreiten 22
to invite einladen 44
invoice Rechnung 59
invoice number Rechnungsnummer 10
to involve umfassen 26
involved in beteiligt an 9
irritant reizend, reizauslösend 49
issue Thema 64
to issue ausstellen, anfertigen 59
item Artikel, Posten 32

J

job fair Jobmesse 13
job interview Vorstellungsgespräch 44
joiner Tischler(in), Schreiner(in) 63

K

to keep (be)halten 40
to keep cool kühl lagern 19
to keep dry trocken lagern 19
knee Knie 26

L

label Aufkleber, Aufschrift 10
to label etikettieren, kennzeichnen, beschriften 19, 50, 64
labour-intensive arbeitsintensiv 33
landfill Mülldeponie 65
lashing Verschnürung 51
layer Schicht 42
leading führend 45
leak undichte Stelle 28
to leak (out) auslaufen 50, 67
lesser geringer 36
letter of application Bewerbungsschreiben 46
licence fee Lizenzgebühr 65
to lift (hoch)heben 26
lifting cart Hubwagen 24, 32
light leicht 24
lightweight leicht(gewichtig) 42
likely wahrscheinlich 20
line *(hier:)* Branche 28
liquid Flüssigkeit 48
liquid chemical flüssige Chemikalie 18
load Last 26
to load (ver)laden 56
loading dock Ladedock 56
load space Ladefläche 43
to load up beladen, aufladen 32
to locate (wieder) finden 16
to log on sich anmelden, sich einwählen 69
to look into sth. einer Sache nachgehen 69
loose lose, locker 27
loss Verlust 9

M

N

O

P

preparation Vorbereitung 60
to prepare vorbereiten 61
pressure Druck 42
to prevent vermeiden 26
price reduction Preisnachlass 69
production area Fertigungsbereich 25
profitability Rentabilität 15
prohibition sign Verbotsschild 50
promptly sofort 36
propane Propan(gas) 49
properly richtig 16, 26
property (Grund-)Besitz, Eigentum 48
to protect schützen, bewahren 64
protective clothing Schutzkleidung 48
protective overall Schutzanzug 48
to provide versorgen 19
punctual pünktlich 45
purchasing (department) Einkauf(sabteilung) 9, 21
purpose (Verwendungs-)Zweck 40

Q

quality department Qualitätsabteilung 9
quantitative mengenmäßig 8
quay parking Parken am richtigen Ablageort 8
query (Such-)Anfrage 19

R

rack Regal 16
rarely selten 23
ratchet Knarre 20
raw materials Rohstoffe 21
R&D (Research and Development) Forschungs- und Entwicklungsabteilung 21
to reach an agreement eine Vereinbarung treffen 58
reason Grund 60
to reassure beruhigen 71
receipt of stock Wareneingang 19
receiving department Warenannahme 9
receiving dock Empfangsrampe 8
receiving note Empfangsbescheinigung 10
receiving staff Personal zuständig für den Wareneingang 9
recently kürzlich 45
to recommend empfehlen 37
to recruit rekrutieren, anstellen 21
recycling plant Recyclinganlage 64
redo noch einmal machen 69
refrigerator wagon Kühlwaggon 57
regardless of ungeachtet, unabhängig von 20
regulation Vorschrift, Bestimmung 67
to reinforce verstärken, betonen 61
relationship Beziehung 52
reliable zuverlässig 36
reliably zuverlässig 25
to remain bleiben 30
to rent verleihen 65
repetitive monoton, sich wiederholend 26
to replace ersetzen 36
to report to unterstehen 23
request Bitte 30
to require benötigen 38
required erforderlich, verlangt, erwünscht 60
to resist widerstehen, standhalten 50
responsibility Verantwortung 22
responsible verantwortlich 45
to retrieve wiederfinden 25
return Rücklieferung, Rücksendung 19
returnable system Rücknahmesystem 65
robot Roboter 24
robust stabil 62
roller conveyor Rollenbahn 25
to roll off wegrollen 51
rope Band 42
routing method elektronisches System zur Übermittlung von Aufträgen 35
rubber Gummi 17

S

safety boots Sicherheitsschuhe 48
safety can Sicherheitsflasche, -kanister 50
safety controlled sicherheitsüberwacht 18
safety precaution Sicherheitsvorkehrung 48
safety rule Sicherheitsvorschrift 43
salesperson Verkäufer(in) 32
sales pitch Verkaufspräsentation 60
salutation *(Brief:)* Anrede 37
sample Muster 37
schedule Zeitplan 56
screwdriver Schraubendreher 38
seaworthy seefest 57
to secure (ab)sichern, schützen 42
securely sicher 48
securing means sichernde Maßnahme(n) 51
sequential order picking auftragsorientierte, serielle Kommissionierung 33
serious ernsthaft 26
service Dienstleistung 60
sewage Abwasser 67
to shape formen, fräsen 22
shelf Regal 16
shelving rack Fachregal 17
shift Schicht 22
shiny glänzend 62
to ship versenden, verschiffen 56
shipping Versand 19
side order Beilage 55
to sign unterschreiben 44
signature Unterschrift 10
significantly bedeutend 35
simultaneously gleichzeitig 34
size Größe 25
skill Fähigkeit 44
slippery rutschig 51
smooth ruhig 26
socket Steckdose, Stecknuss 31, 38
softwood Weichholz 63
solid Feststoff 48
solid stabil 25
solid waste Feststoffabfall 67
solution Lösung 28
to solve lösen 71
to sort sortieren 34
sound Ton, Klang, Geräusch 67
space Platz, Raum 41
spare part Ersatzteil 57
specific bestimmt, spezifisch 69
specification Angabe, Beschreibung 9

T

U

V

W

Bildquellenverzeichnis

4 Thinkstock (Jupiterimages), München; **4** shutterstock (Marcin Balcerzak), New York, NY; **4** BigStockPhoto.com (italianestro), Davis, CA; **5** Thinkstock (iStockphoto), München; **5** iStockphoto (Sean Locke), Calgary, Alberta; **6** LinguaTV GmbH, Berlin; **6** Video(s) supplied by BBC Motion Gallery, London; **6** ZDF, Mainz; **6** ZDF Enterprises GmbH, Mainz; **8** dreamstime.com (Phartisan), Brentwood, TN; **8** Thinkstock (Jupiterimages), München; **8** Thinkstock (iStockphoto), München; **11** Fotolia.com (Anatoly Vartanov), New York; **12** iStockphoto (daniel rodriguez), Calgary, Alberta; **12** Thinkstock (Stockbyte), München; **12** iStockphoto (David Jones), Calgary, Alberta; **12** iStockphoto (Helder Almeida), Calgary, Alberta; **14** iStockphoto (Dean Mitchell), Calgary, Alberta; **15** iStockphoto (4x6), Calgary, Alberta; **16** BigStockPhoto.com (kadmy), Davis, CA; **17** dreamstime.com (Daleen Loest), Brentwood, TN; **17** dreamstime.com (Cebas1), Brentwood, TN; **17** dreamstime.com (Baloncici), Brentwood, TN; **18** dreamstime.com (Angelo Gilardelli), Brentwood, TN; **18** BigStockPhoto.com (fotomy), Davis, CA; **18** dreamstime.com (Frenta), Brentwood, TN; **19** dreamstime.com (Vrcraft), Brentwood, TN; **20** shutterstock (Dmitry Kalinovsky), New York, NY; **20** Thinkstock (BananaStock), München; **20** iStockphoto (sturti), Calgary, Alberta; **20** Thinkstock (iStockphoto), München; **22** shutterstock (Dmitry Kalinovsky), New York, NY; **23** iStockphoto (mediaphotos), Calgary, Alberta; **24** BigStockPhoto.com (kadmy), Davis, CA; **24** iStockphoto (MotoEd), Calgary, Alberta; **24** iStockphoto (gradisca), Calgary, Alberta; **24** Thinkstock (Jupiterimages), München; **25** Thinkstock (Jupiterimages), München; **27** Thinkstock (Photos.com), München; **28** iStockphoto (diego cervo), Calgary, Alberta; **28** iStockphoto (nolimitpictures), Calgary, Alberta; **28** Thinkstock (Wavebreak Media), München; **28** PantherMedia GmbH (Benis Arapovic), München; **30** iStockphoto (PeskyMonkey), Calgary, Alberta; **32** shutterstock (Marcin Balcerzak), New York, NY; **33** shutterstock (auremar), New York, NY; **35** Thinkstock (Creatas), München; **36** iStockphoto (David Jones), Calgary, Alberta; **36** iStockphoto (Warwick Lister-Kaye), Calgary, Alberta; **36** shutterstock (Stephen Coburn), New York, NY; **36** shutterstock (rangizzz), New York, NY; **40** BigStockPhoto.com (italianestro), Davis, CA; **40** Thinkstock (Hemera), München; **40** iStockphoto (subjug), Calgary, Alberta; **41** Fotolia.com (Fotoali), New York; **41** shutterstock (Elena Larina), New York, NY; **41** iStockphoto (RF/Tschakert), Calgary, Alberta; **41** shutterstock (Richard Welter), New York, NY; **41** MEV Verlag GmbH, Augsburg; **41** iStockphoto (sumbul), Calgary, Alberta; **42** BigStockPhoto.com (AardLumens), Davis, CA; **42** iStockphoto (WestLight), Calgary, Alberta; **42** BigStockPhoto.com (ladylike4), Davis, CA; **42** BigStockPhoto.com (mcfields), Davis, CA; **42** BigStockPhoto.com (cphoto), Davis, CA; **42** BigStockPhoto.com (ccaetano), Davis, CA; **43** shutterstock (VoodooDot), New York, NY; **44** shutterstock (Minerva Studio), New York, NY; **44** iStockphoto (Brian Jackson), Calgary, Alberta; **44** shutterstock (StockLite), New York, NY; **44** iStockphoto (Willie B. Thomas), Calgary, Alberta; **46** shutterstock (Goodluz), New York, NY; **48** Fotolia.com (Dr. Jan), New York; **48** BigStockPhoto.com (pixpack), Davis, CA; **49** shutterstock (Bakelyt), New York, NY; **49** Fotolia.com (ufotopixl10), New York; **50** Thinkstock (iStockphoto), München; **50** shutterstock (Bakelyt), New York, NY; **51** dreamstime.com (Leonidikan), Brentwood, TN; **52** iStockphoto (fatihhoca), Calgary, Alberta; **52** iStockphoto (Clerkenwell_Images), Calgary, Alberta; **52** Thinkstock (Purestock), München; **52** iStockphoto (Chris Schmidt), Calgary, Alberta; **53** Thinkstock (BananaStock), München; **54** Thinkstock (Stockbyte), München; **55** iStockphoto (kristian sekulic), Calgary, Alberta; **56** dreamstime.com (Soleg1974), Brentwood, TN; **56** Thinkstock (iStockphoto), München; **56** dreamstime.com (Sfagnan), Brentwood, TN; **57** Thinkstock (iStockphoto), München; **58** dreamstime.com (Alain Lacroix), Brentwood, TN; **59** shutterstock (Diego Cervo), New York, NY; **60** iStockphoto (Clerkenwell_Images), Calgary, Alberta; **60** shutterstock (wavebreakmedia ltd), New York, NY; **60** Thinkstock (Purestock), München; **60** iStockphoto (Oleg Prikhodko), Calgary, Alberta; **61** iStockphoto (bluecinema), Calgary, Alberta; **63** iStockphoto (Joshua Hodge Photography), Calgary, Alberta; **64** BigStockPhoto.com (JustASC), Davis, CA; **64** BigStockPhoto.com (lwzfoto), Davis, CA; **64** Thinkstock (Hemera), München; **64** Thinkstock (Comstock), München; **65** Duales System Deutschland GmbH, Köln-Porz-Eil; **66** Fotolia.com (industrieblick), New York; **67** Thinkstock (iStockphoto), München; **68** iStockphoto (YanLev), Calgary, Alberta; **68** iStockphoto (Steve Debenport), Calgary, Alberta; **68** iStockphoto (Sean Locke), Calgary, Alberta; **68** iStockphoto (Louis-Paul St-Onge), Calgary, Alberta; **69** iStockphoto (Sean Locke), Calgary, Alberta; **72** LinguaTV GmbH, Berlin; **73** LinguaTV GmbH, Berlin; **74** ZDF Enterprises GmbH, Mainz; **75** ZDF Enterprises GmbH, Mainz; **76** ZDF, Mainz; **76** ZDF Enterprises GmbH, Mainz; **77** Video(s) supplied by BBC Motion Gallery, London; **118** Klett-Archiv, Stuttgart; **COVER** Getty Images RF (OJO Images), München; **COVER** Getty Images (Blend Images), München

Sollte es in einem Einzelfall nicht gelungen sein, den korrekten Rechteinhaber ausfindig zu machen, so werden berechtigte Ansprüche selbstverständlich im Rahmen der üblichen Regelungen abgegolten.

Textquellenverzeichnis

81/82 Source: Powered Hand Tools – Pneumatic Tools – Basic Safety, http://www.ccohs.ca/oshanswers/safety_haz/power_tools/pneumat.html, Canadian Centre of Occupational Health and Safety (CCOHS), year of publication. Reproduced with the permission of CCOHS, 2012.